Women's Rights at Work

Women's Rights at Work

A Handbook of Employment Law

Alison Clarke

Pluto Press

LONDON • STERLING, VIRGINIA

First published 2001 by Pluto Press
345 Archway Road, London N6 5AA
and 22883 Quicksilver Drive, Sterling, VA 20166–2012, USA

www.plutobooks.com

British Library Cataloguing in Publication Data
A catalogue record for this book is available from the British Library

Library of Congress Cataloging-in-Publication Data applied for

ISBN   0 7453 1564 X hardback
          0 7453 1559 3 paperback

10	09	08	07	06	05	04	03	02	01
10	9	8	7	6	5	4	3	2	1

Designed and produced for Pluto Press by
Chase Publishing Services, Fortescue, Sidmouth EX10 9QG
Typeset from disk by Gawcott Typesetting Services
Printed in the European Union by Antony Rowe, Chippenham, England

This book is dedicated to the memory of Pauline Turkie,
a woman who was not afraid to assert her rights.

Acknowledgements

I would like to thank Mary Stacey, a solicitor, part-time employment tribunal chairman and deputy chairman of the Central Arbitration Committee, for all her help in checking the accuracy of this book. Thanks also to Jacksons Solicitors, in particular to Kevin Fletcher, for giving me access to the material needed to produce the book.

Finally, I would like to thank my partner John and son Aaron for their patience during the time that I have been engrossed in writing the book.

Contents

List of Abbreviations   x

Introduction   1

1 **Finding a Job**   5
   Advertisements   5
   Recruitment   8
   References   20
   Convictions   22
   Withdrawal of Job Offer   23
   Medical Testing   24

2 **Getting Started**   26
   The Contract of Employment   26
   Employment Status   30
   Employment of Women from Overseas   36

3 **Equality in the Workplace**   39
   Equal Pay   40
   Discrimination in Pay Systems   47
   Maternity Rights   48
   Part-time Workers   57
   Job Sharers   61
   Sex and Race Discrimination   61
   Disability Discrimination   72
   Transsexuals   82
   Sexual Orientation   82

Age Discrimination   83
Promotion, Transfer and Training under the SDA
    and RRA   85
Promotion, Transfer and Training under the DDA   88
Family Friendly Policies   89

4 **Conduct and Rights at Work**   92
Contract of Employment   92
Deductions from Wages   94
National Minimum Wage Act 1998   98
Trade Union Rights   105
Other Public Duties   112
Job Mobility   114
Office Romances   117
Clothing and Appearance   118
Searches, Surveillance and Drug Testing   121
Sickness at Work   125
Data Protection Act 1998   130
Human Rights Act 1998   134

5 **Health and Safety at Work**   136
The Common Law   136
Domestic Legislation   137
European Legislation   138
Working Time Regulations   146
Violence at Work   157
Working at Home and Working Alone   158
Bullying and Harassment at Work   159
Stress at Work   166

6 **Dismissal**   169
Unfair Dismissal   169
Constructive Dismissal   173
Wrongful Dismissal   175
Summary Dismissal   176
Redundancy   177
Notice Period   189
Effective Date of Termination (EDT)   191
Whistleblowing   191

7 **Post-employment Problems**   196
   Claims and Representation   196
   Making a Claim   197
   At the Hearing   209
   Remedies and Compensation   211

8 **General**   216
   Useful Addresses   216
   References   219
   Table of Cases   219
   Table of Statutes   223
   Table of Regulations   223

Index   225

List of Abbreviations

ACAS   Advisory, Conciliation and Arbitration Service
ALL ER All England Law Reports
CH   Chancery Division
COET   Central Office of Employment Tribunals
CRE   Commission for Racial Equality
DRC   Disability Rights Commission
DTI   Department of Trade and Industry
EAT   Employment Appeal Tribunal
ECJ   European Court of Justice
EOC   Equal Opportunities Commission
EOR   Equal Opportunities Review
EqPA   Equal Pay Act
ERA   Employment Rights Act
GOQ   Genuine Occupational Qualification
ICR   Industrial Cases Reports
IRLR   Industrial Relations Law Reports
JES   Job Evaluation Scheme
RRA   Race Relations Act
SDA   Sex Discrimination Act
SMP   Statutory Maternity Pay

Introduction

Women have the same legal rights at work as men. At least, that's the theory. There are, after all, no statutes which only apply to men, no legislation which is gender specific to them. If anything, the opposite is true. For instance, women benefit from maternity rights which, by definition, do not apply to men. Men cannot have six months off work, get paid for some of it and then demand their old job back.

So why a book about women's employment rights? Simply because women suffer more problems in the workplace than men; problems such as low pay, discrimination and occupational segregation. For instance, despite the numbers of women in the workplace in the twenty-first century, they still earn, on average, far less than men. A statistic that holds true after 25 years of equal pay legislation.

Why, then, are the problems so intractable? It is beyond the remit of this book to analyse the reasons for women's inequality at work, but one issue is clear: women need to work flexibly. For instance, they need to take maternity leave, possibly more than once, requiring their employer to find (and pay for) a replacement who has to be dismissed when the woman wants to return.

But women also have other problems to contend with. Although there are men who juggle work with domestic commitments, it is women, on the whole, who shoulder the principal responsibility for combining work and the family. As a result, they often need to work part time or at the very least have the option of working flexibly if those commitments are to be fulfilled.

As a result, because of the inflexible way in which work is structured, many employers prefer to hire men, not least because they do not take maternity leave. Employers also carry around their own set of prejudices. For instance, many seem to think that men are stronger/more reliable/more likely to 'fit in' to the existing workforce. If the job requires a degree of physical fitness, employers often take the view that only a man can do the job.

There are, of course, exceptions to the rule. Employers are happy enough to employ women who are prepared to work for peanuts, often on a part-time basis. Hence the segregation of women in low-paid occupations such as cleaners, nurses, homeworkers, etc.; occupations which are, incidentally, some of the most vulnerable to occupational violence. In general, it is women who are most likely to be harassed, bullied or suffer violence in the workplace.

The workplace can, therefore, be a very hostile environment for women. Hence the introduction of legislation, like the Sex Discrimination Act and the Equal Pay Act, to protect them (although it applies equally to men) from some of the more overt discrimination they have had to put up with. Unfortunately, some of the legislation has turned out to be so tortuous in its implementation – the Equal Pay Act springs to mind – that it has still had little or no effect on the working environment for women.

The outcome of all this is that women often do not have the time or the inclination to find out about their rights at work. However, if they are to survive and assert themselves at work, they need to become aware of their rights and be prepared to assert them. And that means all of them – not just the basic right not to be discriminated against when trying to find a job. It means asserting the right to work in a safe environment, the right not to be bullied at work, the right to have time off for training, the right to promotion, the right to equal pay.

This book aims to ensure that women are familiar with all their rights. Although it looks in detail at discrimination, maternity rights and equal pay, it is not restricted to that 'ghetto'. Nor does it take a legalistic approach to women's employment rights. Rather than describing and explaining how various laws can be used individually to protect women from discrimination in the workplace, the book turns that approach on its head. Instead, it considers the problem from the woman's point of view by looking at the context in which she works and by applying individual pieces of legislation to problems which may arise in those situations.

Basically, the book follows a 'cradle-to-grave' approach. It begins by exploring the potential problems facing women trying to find a job and ends with an examination of how to pursue a claim for unfair dismissal. It gives practical advice and tips for most workplace problems likely to confront women. For example, it will help women know what to do if their employer:

- Asks discriminatory questions at an interview
- Changes their contract without consulting them
- Pays them less than a man
- Dismisses them because they are pregnant
- Discriminates against them because they work part time
- Makes them redundant because they were one of the last to be hired
- Refuses to give them a reference

The book also provides a handy checklist of dates by which certain claims have to be made, thereby ensuring that deadlines are not missed. It also provides a list of addresses of useful organisations, in the event that further information is needed.

Of course, women do not have to resort to litigation every time they want to persuade their employer of their rights. What is useful, however, is to be familiar with them to give women the confidence to assert themselves. The law is, in fact, a very crude weapon which should only be used as a last resort once a woman has exhausted all possible negotiations with her employer and preferably with the help of her trade union.

This book will have served its purpose if it gives women the confidence to assert their rights and to challenge their employer, when appropriate. The very fact that you stand up for yourself is enough to send a message to your employer that, although you are a woman, you are no pushover. All women have the right to be treated fairly at work. Make sure that you're one of them.

1
Finding a Job

Finding a job is not the easiest thing in the world – a quick look at the unemployment figures in the UK will testify to that. Unfortunately for women, the search may not be entirely straight-forward – there are plenty of employers who either do not want to employ women or who will only do so if they can hire them on a lower wage than men. For disabled and ethnic minority women, the problem is even more acute.

There are, of course, a few individuals (usually men) who never have to look for a job – people with so many skills whom employers are prepared to headhunt from other firms, usually with the lure of extra cash. Lucky them, you might think. But the practice raises a more important consideration than just straightforward envy. And that is whether it is legal for employers not to advertise.

Advertisements

Is it Legal Not to Advertise a Job?

Unfortunately, there is no obligation on employers to advertise a vacancy. But even though they cannot be made to advertise, it may be discriminatory if they do not. (See Chapter 3 for an explanation of direct and indirect discrimination.)

For instance, in a recent case brought by a solicitor against the Lord Chancellor (*Coker and Osamor* v. *Lord Chancellor and Lord Chancellor's Department*), the employment tribunal said that the Lord Chancellor had indirectly discriminated against Ms Coker.

This was because he picked someone from among his own circle of (male) friends without advertising the post.

Likewise the sex discrimination case brought by a barrister, Josephine Hayes, against the Attorney General (*Hayes* v. *Attorney General*) for the way in which he appointed a male government lawyer. Because the post was not advertised – the successful candidate was chosen from a secret list of approved barristers – Ms Hayes claimed she was overlooked in favour of male colleagues. Although the claim was settled out of court, the Attorney General accepted that informal consultation may lead to indirect discrimination.

Does the Advertisement Discriminate against you under the SDA or RRA?

Once employers decide to advertise, they have to make sure that the advert does not contravene the Sex Discrimination Act or the Race Relations Act. Basically, the law says that the advert should not refer to the gender of the person the employer is looking for, nor their ethnic origin. So, for instance, adverts for 'salesgirls' or 'firemen' are out; so are adverts which suggest that people with certain racial backgrounds will be excluded. There are a few exceptions to this rule and these are considered in the next section of this chapter.

So if you see an advert which seems to discriminate against you in this way, contact the Equal Opportunities Commission or the Commission for Racial Equality, the only bodies entitled to bring proceedings under this section (although check first that it does not fall into any of the exceptions explained below).

Advertisements for staff described as self-employed are also covered by the advertising provisions of the Sex Discrimination Act. The same principle would apply equally to the Race Relations Act.

What about the DDA?

The Disability Discrimination Act – which only applies to employers with 15 or more employees – operates slightly differently. It allows an employer to advertise openly for disabled candidates, with the result that the able-bodied cannot claim that an advert is discriminatory against them. A disabled person can, however, complain to an employment tribunal if an advert infers a bias against the disabled, as long as he or she had applied for the job in question.

Does the Law Sometimes Allow Discriminatory Advertisements under the SDA or RRA?

This section does not apply to the Disability Discrimination Act.

An employer is allowed to discriminate where a person's sex or race is a genuine occupational qualification (GOQ) for the job, in other words, where the employer can show that the job has to be done by someone of a particular sex or race. If that is the case, the law allows the employer to discriminate in recruitment, opportunities for promotion or transfer to, or training for, that job. It follows that if the discrimination is lawful under the Sex Discrimination Act or Race Relations Act, so is the advertisement.

A GOQ may only be claimed in the following circumstances under the Sex Discrimination Act:

- *Physiology or authenticity*: for example, a job as a model or an actor
- *Decency or privacy*: for example, a job which is likely to involve physical contact or where people may be undressing
- *Living in*: the jobholder is living, or working, in a private home where there is a high degree of physical contact
- *Single sex accommodation*: the jobholder has to live in and there is only sleeping or sanitary provision for one sex
- *Single sex establishment*: the job has to be done by one particular sex because it is based in an institution providing special care for one sex only
- *Personal services*: for example, job holders such as rape counsellors, birth control advisers or welfare officers
- *Outside the UK*: the job will involve duties in a country outside the UK, for instance, where the law prevents women from doing certain jobs, such as driving
- *Married couples*: the job is one of two to be held by a married couple

There are four grounds on which race is a GOQ under the Race Relations Act:

- *Dramatic performance*: it is worth noting that this exception only applies to skin colour – it is quite acceptable under the Act for, say, an English actor to play the part of an Irish person (however annoying it might be to the Irish)

- *Authenticity*: the job involves being an artist's or photographic model
- *Restaurants*: the job involves working in a place where food and drink are served to the public, such as a waiter in a Chinese or Indian restaurant
- *Personal services*: the job holder provides people of a particular racial group with personal welfare services

Is it Unlawful for an Employer to Give Instructions to Discriminate?

It is unlawful under both the Sex Discrimination Act and the Race Relations Act for an employer to instruct an employment agency or job centre to carry out an unlawful, discriminatory act. For instance, it is unlawful for an employer to tell a job centre not to send 'any coloureds or foreigners' for interview. Likewise, it is unlawful for the job centre or employment agency to publish discriminatory advertisements. The same principle would apply to the Disability Discrimination Act.

The employer's intention is irrelevant. An employer would still be in breach of the legislation if, for instance, he or she told a job centre that there was no point in sending women for interview because the job involved lifting.

Recruitment

All three Acts – the Sex Discrimination Act, the Race Relations Act and the Disability Discrimination Act – contain specific measures to try to prohibit discrimination by employers during the recruitment process. There are basically three ways in which it is unlawful for an employer to discriminate at this stage:

- In the arrangements made for deciding who should be offered a job (such as the instructions given to a personnel officer or to an employment agency)
- In any terms of employment (for instance, in relation to pay or holidays)
- By refusing, or deliberately omitting, to offer someone a job (by rejecting an application or by deliberately avoiding consideration of an application)

Have you Been Discriminated against in the Offer of a Job?

There is no statutory definition of what constitutes an 'arrangement' in the recruitment process. Although advertising is not included, just about everything else in the process can be. In other words, the method/s used for recruitment, the job description, the wording on the application form, the way the interview is conducted, the criteria used for selection and even a medical examination (see later in the chapter).

> In a recent race discrimination case (*London Borough of Croydon* v. *Kuttappan*), the Employment Appeal Tribunal said that the concept of 'arrangements' included the following:
> - A refusal to consider an application at all
> - The exclusion of applicants in a particular area
> - Telling potential applicants not to apply for the job
> - Telling an applicant that the job is filled when it is not
> - A refusal to interview a person or to provide an unbiased interviewing panel

This means that any discrimination at any stage of the recruitment process can be challenged long before any offer or refusal of employment has been made. At any of these stages the victim of discrimination can, therefore, bring a claim before an employment tribunal, but it stands to reason that if it can be shown that the applicant was very unlikely to have got the job, then the compensation will be limited. As with advertisements, recruitment arrangements may still be discriminatory even if there was no intention to discriminate.

What Rules Apply to Job Descriptions/Specifications?

There is no legal requirement on an employer to provide a written job description or specification. But if he or she bothers to do so, then it should not fall foul of any of the discrimination legislation; that means it should be written in non-discriminatory terms and should exclude requirements which are not central to the job.

Women should study every job description carefully for any bias in the way the job is set out. For instance, a job description for a driver which emphasises heavy lifting may be a way for employers to filter out women applicants at an early stage. It may be that there is little or no lifting, or that any which has to be done could be done with or by someone else other than the driver.

The Code of Practice for the Disability Discrimination Act says that including unnecessary or marginal requirements, as well as blanket exclusions, in a job description or specification can lead to discrimination. For instance, if an employer refused to employ anyone with epilepsy as a driver – although some have a licence and can get insurance – he or she will probably be guilty of discrimination.

The Equal Opportunities Commission in its Code of Practice recommends the following:

• That employers look at the qualifications and requirements being applied to a job if they seem to inhibit applications from one particular sex (or married people). They should only be retained if justified for doing the job
• That age limits should be scrapped, unless necessary for the job. Although age discrimination is not unlawful in this country, an unjustifiable age limit could constitute unlawful indirect discrimination, for example, against women who have taken time out of employment for childcare purposes

What about Application Forms in Terms of Sex and Race Discrimination?

Application forms should not ask irrelevant questions about a person's sex or race. For instance, employers should not ask about the marital status of an applicant, unless they can show the relevance of the questions to the job. If the questions are relevant for whatever reason, they must be applied equally to all candidates, irrespective of gender.

In its Code of Practice, the Commission for Racial Equality recommends that employers should not demand a higher level of educational qualification than is needed. In particular, it says that employers should not disqualify applicants because they cannot complete an application form in English themselves, unless that would constitute a valid test of the standard of English required for the job.

For instance, in a case brought against British Leyland (*Isa and Rashid* v. *BL Cars Ltd*), two Pakistani applicants were refused employment because they could not complete their application forms themselves. BL subsequently admitted that the requirement to complete complex forms was unlikely to be necessary for the labouring jobs they were applying for.

What about Application Forms in Terms of Disability Discrimination?

Under the Disability Discrimination Act, the employer can do the following:

- Include questions on the application form asking whether the applicant is disabled
- Ask whether the applicant may need special arrangements to be made in the event that the disabled candidate is asked for interview (see later in this chapter under reasonable adjustments)

In addition under the Disability Discrimination Act, it may also be reasonable:

- To expect an employer to provide information about jobs in alternative formats, such as Braille or on computer disc, if there is time to do so and it could easily be done
- To expect an employer to make a reasonable adjustment to cope with an application form submitted in a different medium – for instance, an application on tape or made over the telephone

What Selection Criteria Should Employers Use?

The whole issue of selection criteria is fraught with problems, mainly because many employers are not aware that by failing to adopt objective and transparent procedures they may be discriminating unconsciously. For instance, employers who do not decide appropriate selection criteria in advance for shortlisting purposes are likely to rely on their own value judgements when sifting application forms, thereby potentially denying suitable candidates the chance of an interview.

In its Code of Practice, the Commission for Racial Equality recommends that:

- Employers do not demand a standard of English higher than that needed to do the job

- That employers do not impose a requirement for UK qualifications. It says that overseas degrees, diplomas and other qualifications which are comparable with UK qualifications should be acceptable as equivalents and not simply assumed to be inferior
- Employers examine their selection criteria and tests to make sure that they relate to the requirements of the job. For instance, it says that selection tests that contain irrelevant questions or exercises on issues likely to be unfamiliar to racial minority candidates should not be used. This might include general knowledge questions on subjects familiar only to indigenous applicants

In some instances, it is more obvious than others that an employer is operating a discriminatory policy. In one case (*Hurley v. Mustoe*), the employer had a policy of not employing women with children. Not surprisingly, the Employment Appeal Tribunal found that this was discriminatory against women.

Is there Evidence of Discrimination in the Selection Criteria?

For the applicant herself, the problems in proving discrimination at this stage can be significant, but not insurmountable. What you need is evidence. If you decide to bring a claim, it is important to amass as much supporting material as possible:

- Ask the employer for the selection criteria used for shortlisting and the results for each candidate. A tribunal is unlikely to be impressed by an employer who is unable to provide any
- Ask the employer for the scoring results of each candidate at the interview (these can be given anonymously if necessary) and details of how those results were arrived at. You can do this in a questionnaire (see Chapter 7 for details).

How do you Get the Evidence?

If the employer refuses to produce the necessary documentation and you have to make an application to the tribunal to make the employer cough up (a process known as 'discovery'), the tribunal is likely to grant your request as long as the documents you are asking for are relevant to proving your claim and would not involve the employer in too much work in getting them for you. However, in order to start this process, you need to have already lodged a claim with the tribunal. See Chapter 7 for more details.

For instance, in the Josephine Hayes case against the Attorney General (see above), the tribunal said that even the 'secret soundings' between a number of very senior law officers were 'discoverable'. This is very significant because it means that if you know that there have been secret consultations as part of the selection process you can ask the tribunal to order disclosure of them.

What about Aptitude Tests?

Aptitude tests have the same potential for discrimination as any other tests, although used correctly they can reduce bias in the selection process. The Disability Discrimination Act Code of Practice warns that although employers are not prevented from carrying out aptitude tests under the Act, routine testing of all candidates may discriminate against some individuals. In that case, employers should revise the tests to take account of specific disabled candidates. For instance, in the case of an employer who uses numeracy tests in every selection, irrespective of the job, if the specific job involves little or no work with numbers, the employer should make a 'reasonable adjustment' (see later in this chapter) for a candidate with learning difficulties who fails the test, by waiving that particular requirement.

Women who think they have been discriminated against at this stage should ask the employer for the results of their own tests and those of the other applicants.

What Questions Should an Employer Ask at Interview?

The Equal Opportunities Commission says that questions at interview should relate to the requirements of the job. If it is necessary to assess whether personal circumstances will affect performance of the job, this should be discussed without detailed questions being asked about marital status, children and domestic obligations. Questions about marriage plans or family intentions should not be asked as they are likely to show a bias against women. The Equal Opportunities Commission also points out that employers can obtain the information they need for personnel records after a job offer has been made.

So, for instance, in an interview for a job which requires some overseas travel, an employer can ask a woman whether she would be able to comply with that requirement as long as he or she asks all other candidates the same questions. What the employer should not do is cross-examine the woman about her personal circumstances, such as asking whether she is married and has children.

In real life, however, it may be difficult to prove a link between questions asked at interview and failure to get the job.

What Questions Should Not Be Asked at Interview about your Family Life?

The Equal Opportunities Commission has collated a list of questions about a woman's domestic life which should not be asked, such as:

- What is your marital status?
- Do you have children?
- If so, how many and what are their ages?
- What is your husband's employment?
- Do you have a boyfriend?
- Are you planning to get engaged/married/have children?

However, it is worth noting that although questions about a woman's domestic arrangements will generally be discriminatory, there are exceptions. For instance, a woman lost her claim against Strathclyde Regional Council (*Adams* v. *Strathclyde Regional Council*) despite the fact that it had asked her how many children she had and what their ages were. In this particular case, the Employment Appeal Tribunal decided that the employer had asked the questions to put the woman at her ease and they could equally have been asked of a man.

Amazingly, in another case (*Mrs J Woodhead* v. *Chief Constable of West Yorkshire Police*) the Employment Appeal Tribunal said that it was acceptable to ask a woman questions about her family life because she was applying for a job with the police. This was necessary, apparently, because the job involved discipline and a code of behaviour which put the duties of the office before private interest. Male applicants were not asked similar questions. It's a pity that the applicant did not appeal against this dubious finding.

Although the case law can be confusing (and, on occasions, contradictory), the general rule remains that if an employer asks you questions about your family or domestic life, they are very likely to be discriminatory. If you feel aggrieved, you should lodge a claim with an employment tribunal (see Chapter 7).

What Medical Questions Should Not Be Asked at Interview?

The Equal Opportunities Commission also recommends that the following medical questions should not be asked:

- Do you suffer from period pains?
- Have you ever taken time off work owing to period pains?
- Have you ever taken time off work owing to 'female ailments'?
- Do you suffer from any gynaecological abnormalities?
- Are you pregnant?
- Do you intend to become pregnant?
- Have you ever had a baby?

The Commission recommends that if medical information is required by an employer, then more neutral questions would be acceptable. For instance, it would be okay to ask a woman whether she suffers from any medical condition which might affect her performance in the job. Likewise, it is acceptable to ask job applicants for their sickness record over the last twelve months or so. These questions are only acceptable if they are asked equally of men and women and relate to specific job requirements.

Even where the work involves special hazards for women who might become pregnant (see Chapter 5) such as working with ionising radiation or lead, employers should still not use application forms or employment interviews to try to identify women who might fall into that category. That information can be obtained during the course of a regular medical examination by a qualified medical adviser, in the same way that a person's health might be checked before appointment (see later in this chapter).

There are also questions which, although not discriminatory in themselves, may still infer a discriminatory attitude on the part of the employer.

For instance, a woman who applied for the position of a golf professional was asked, 'Do you think men respond as well to a woman golf professional as to a man?' (*Saunders* v. *Richmond-upon-Thames*). The Employment Appeal Tribunal decided that the question was not unlawful in this instance, but that it was always necessary to look at the circumstances of each case and the purpose for which the question was asked. So although the question may not be discriminatory in itself, it could be evidence of a final decision that was.

What Questions Can Be Asked of a Disabled Person at Interview?

There are a number of rules which apply under the Disability Discrimination Act:

- Employers are allowed to ask about a person's disability at interview, but if they do, they must not use the information to discriminate against the disabled person
- Employers should only ask about a disability if it is relevant to the person's ability to do the job
- Asking about the effects of a disability may help the employer to decide what adjustments he or she needs to make, assuming the disabled person was to be offered the job

The Act does not prevent a disabled person from keeping the fact of her disability confidential. If the employer subsequently dismisses her for deceit, she can argue that the dismissal is for a reason related to her disability and therefore constitutes discrimination (unless there were any health and safety risks involved).

What Reasonable Adjustments Should an Employer Make for a Disabled Person?

To avoid placing a disabled job applicant (or existing employee) at a disadvantage at interview the Disability Discrimination Act says that every employer with more than 15 employees must:

- Make a reasonable adjustment to the physical set-up of the premises if the person is placed at a substantial disadvantage

• Make a reasonable adjustment to the arrangements made for a job interview. Not surprisingly, this obligation only arises where the employer knows (or should have known) that the applicant had a disability
• Find out whether the candidate's disability might place her at a disadvantage at interview, although this obligation has its limits

For instance, in one case (*Rideout* v. *TC Group*) the applicant suffered from a rare form of light sensitive epilepsy. Although the employer had been made aware of her disability, he did not realise that he should have adjusted the lighting in the room. Because the employer could not have been expected to know what adjustments to make, the Employment Appeal Tribunal held that he did not discriminate against the applicant.

To avoid these problems, employers should think ahead for interviews and ask applicants whether any special arrangements need to be made. Depending on your disability, you might want to suggest a number of simple alterations such as ensuring that the interviewer faces you if you have a hearing impairment, or that the interview takes place in a room which is wheelchair accessible. If the employer seems resistant to your suggestions, you may have a claim for discrimination if you have been put at a disadvantage by the employer's refusal to make reasonable adjustments.

Equally, job applicants need to consider letting the prospective employer know of any potential difficulties and perhaps suggest what adjustments need to be made.

What about Discrimination in Offers of Employment?

It is against the law for an employer to discriminate against a woman in the terms on which he or she offers her employment. This section only covers *offers* of employment and not the terms and conditions which apply once an applicant is in post which are covered elsewhere by the legislation (see Chapter 3).

There are very few claims of discrimination under this heading as most employers tend not to offer the job at all to the woman rather than offering it to her on blatantly different terms to that of a man. Either that or the woman is not aware of the discrimination until she is in the post. As this section only applies to job offers, the aggrieved woman would have to have been offered the job in the first place. Under the Disability Discrimination Act, an employer can defeat a discrimination claim if he or she can justify offering a less favourable contract to a disabled person (see Chapter 3 for more details).

What if the Employer Refuses to Make an Offer of Employment?

All three Acts – the Race Relations Act, the Sex Discrimination Act and the Disability Discrimination Act – state that it is unlawful for an employer to discriminate against a woman by refusing to offer her a job or by deliberately omitting to offer her a job. There is no legal requirement on an employer to tell an applicant why she has been unsuccessful, but you can always ask for the reasons in your discrimination questionnaire (see Chapter 7 for an explanation). If the employer refuses to answer them or is evasive, the tribunal is likely to assume the worst of the employer – otherwise known as an 'adverse inference'.

It can be difficult for an applicant to a tribunal to show that, had it not been for the discriminatory attitude of the employer, she would have been given the job. The most obvious situations are those where the applicant is told that the vacancy has been filled, only to discover that it is still available to men or white people.

For instance, a West Indian woman who applied in person at a hotel was told the job had been taken. When she telephoned later, she was told it was still available (*Scott* v. *Norfolk House Hotel*). The same thing happened in the case of Mr Hussain (*Hussain* v. *Alfred Brown (Worsted Mills) Ltd*) who applied unsuccessfully for a job in a textile mill near his home in Bradford. His son then applied under the name of Taylor and was offered a trial by the company.

In such claims, the tribunal will look at each aspect of the recruitment process to see if there has been any bias against the applicant. For instance, if a woman has been passed over in favour of a man with lower qualifications, the tribunal will want to examine the criteria used for selection to see if they were discriminatory. It is important to note that it is not automatically discriminatory for an employer to pick a man who, on paper, is less well qualified than a woman.

Finally, a refusal to employ, or to offer employment, to a woman because she is pregnant which might, in turn, cause the employer possible financial hardship is clear sex discrimination (*Dekker* v. *Stichting Vormingscentrum voor Jonge Volwassen (VJV Centrum) Plus*).

What about Positive Action in Favour of Women?

Positive discrimination (or positive action) means giving preferential treatment to a member of one particular sex or racial group – a policy which some women may think has been operating for far too long in favour of men. However, it generally constitutes discrimination under both the Sex Discrimination Act and the Race Relations Act.

It is, therefore, unlawful, to operate a policy whereby women candidates would be automatically favoured over men in an effort to redress the gender balance, as the Labour Party found out to its cost when one of its members objected to the introduction of all-women shortlists (*Jepson and Dyas-Elliott* v. *The Labour Party and ors*).

But following a number of rulings by the ECJ, it seems that employers can operate a limited policy of positive discrimination in favour of women. The practical result of the decisions is that if, judged against an objective assessment, a man was the best candidate for the job, then he should be appointed despite the positive action policy.

Can you Have Positive Action under the SDA and RRA?

Limited provisions exist under both the Sex Discrimination Act and the Race Relations Act allowing an employer to take positive action in favour of women or a particular racial group to prevent discrimination.

The legislation says that an employer can:

- Provide training to people who have been out of work because of domestic or family responsibilities, such as mothers returning to work
- Offer training to women or members of a particular racial group to help them get work if in the preceding twelve months there were very few of them doing that sort of work

- Offer training to existing employees (as opposed to those looking for work) if in the preceding twelve months there were very few of them doing that sort of work
- Run a discriminatory recruitment campaign to encourage women or members of a particular racial group to apply for certain kinds of work, as long as there were no women (or very few) doing that particular kind of work in the preceding twelve months

For example, an employer with no black supervisors but a high proportion of black assembly line workers can arrange training for black workers seeking promotion. He or she can also advertise for black workers to encourage them to apply for vacancies at that grade or print leaflets in relevant minority languages to encourage them to apply. In addition, an employer can indicate in an advert that training would be made available to those returning to work.

Can you Have Positive Action under the DDA?

Employers are legally required to make reasonable adjustments to work arrangements and the workplace environment to accommodate disabled people if they are substantially disadvantaged by the current arrangements. There is nothing in the Act to stop employers from treating a disabled person more favourably than someone without a disability. That being so, there is no redress under the Disability Discrimination Act for an aggrieved able-bodied person to bring a claim of discrimination against an employer who has allegedly discriminated in favour of a disabled person.

The point of positive action is to ensure that people from previously excluded groups can compete on equal terms with other applicants. It is intended to make up for the accumulated effects of past discrimination. The law does not oblige employers to take positive action, but it allows them to do so.

References

Is there an Obligation on your Employer to Provide a Reference?

There is no specific statute that deals with references, nor is there any obligation on an employer to provide one. However, under case law (that is, law made by judges in court), it has been established that employers must ensure that any reference they give is accurate and truthful. Otherwise you can sue the employer for defamation or negligence (if you can afford to do so).

Does your Employer Have to Let you See the Reference?

No, your employer does not have to let you see the reference. That can be problematic because if you fail to get a job as a result of a poor reference, you will want to see it to challenge its contents. However, the employer may try to argue that the document is confidential and refuse to show it to you. You can ask the court to order discovery of the document (see Chapter 7), but in order to do so you will probably need the help of a lawyer – try your trade union, the local law centre or Citizens Advice Bureau for help.

Alternatively if you can claim discrimination (whether on the basis of sex, race or disability), you could ask to see a copy of the reference using a discrimination questionnaire (see Chapter 7 for details of how to do this).

Whether the court orders discovery will depend on all the circumstances of the case. Under the Data Protection Act 1998, disclosure of a reference *held by* an employer (as opposed to a reference *provided by* an employer) should be made as long as the source cannot be identified. (See Chapter 4 for more details about the Data Protection Act.)

Can you Challenge what a Reference Says?

On the other hand, you may know exactly what it says and want to challenge it.

Take the case of Mr Bartholomew who used to be head of the race equality unit in Hackney (*Bartholomew* v. *London Borough of Hackney*). He was refused a job with a social services department in another London borough after they received a reference from Hackney which said that at the time of leaving he had been the subject of disciplinary action for gross misconduct, but did not give any details of the misconduct nor that Mr Bartholomew had strongly denied the charge.

Mr Bartholomew claimed damages for negligence, arguing that his former employers were in breach of their duty of care in providing a reference which, although factually correct, was unfair to him overall. The Court of Appeal disagreed. It said that, although the reference could have been better, it complied on the whole with the duty on the employer to ensure that a reference should be fair, accurate and true. The court took the view that if Hackney had not mentioned the suspension, the reference might have misled the other borough.

Although Mr Bartholomew lost his case, there is now an obligation on employers, as a result of this decision, to give a 'fair' impression of the employee in any reference. This is a heavier burden than a duty simply to provide an 'accurate and truthful' reference.

Can you Get a Reference even if you are no Longer an Employee?

In a recent case (*Coote* v. *Granada Hospitality Ltd*), Mrs Coote's employers refused to give her a reference because she had brought a discrimination claim against them during her employment. She claimed victimisation and the Employment Appeal Tribunal agreed, saying that she could rely on the Sex Discrimination Act.

It is not clear whether a claim under the Race Relations Act would succeed, but it is certainly worth a try (see also Chapter 3).

Convictions

Do you Have to Disclose a Conviction?

Some application forms contain a section requiring anyone with a conviction to disclose it. This area of the law is governed by the Rehabilitation of Offenders Act 1974 (ROA), which enables some criminal convictions to become 'spent' or forgotten after a rehabilitation period. This is a set period of time from the date of conviction after which an ex-offender is not obliged to mention the conviction when applying for a job. The period after which a conviction becomes spent varies depending on the seriousness of the original crime, but a sentence of over 30 months can never become spent.

What is the Purpose of the ROA?

The purpose of the Act is to provide some protection for ex-offenders by making it unlawful for employers to refuse employment because of a *spent* conviction. However, if asked by a prospective employer whether she has an *unspent* conviction, the woman must disclose it. If she fails to do so and is found out, she may be dismissed on the ground of having deceived the employer. Conversely, if she is not asked about a conviction, she is not under a legal duty to disclose it.

What are the Exceptions to the Act?

There are a number of important exceptions to the Act, such as:

- Youth workers
- Social workers
- Doctors
- Lawyers
- Accountants
- NHS workers
- Probation officers
- Dentists
- Opticians
- Chemists

If the post falls into one of the exceptions, the result is that even if the woman has a *spent* conviction the employer can refuse to offer the post and this will be fair.

Withdrawal of Job Offer

Is it a Breach of Contract to Withdraw the Offer of a Job?

Once a prospective employer has made an unconditional offer and you have accepted it, there will be a breach of the contract if the employer then unilaterally withdraws the offer. Equally, it is a breach of contract for you to withdraw once you have accepted the offer, but it is unlikely that the employer will sue you because of the time and money involved. However, if the offer is withdrawn before you have accepted it, there is nothing you can do about that.

What Should you Do if there is a Breach of Contract?

If you want to sue the employer (and you may if you have handed in your notice or have suffered some other loss), you should make a claim for damages for the breach of contract. This is usually limited to the pay and benefits for the notice period that the employer should have given you to terminate the contract lawfully. You may also want to make a claim for any expenses you have incurred.

If the total sum involved is less than £5,000, the best idea is to make a claim in the Small Claims Court. There are a series of helpful leaflets on how to pursue a small claim produced by the Court Service which you can get from your local county court or Citizens Advice Bureau. If it is more than £5,000, then you have to make a claim for breach of contract to the county court. Again, to do so you may need the help of your local Citizens Advice Bureau or the local court clerk.

Alternatively, you can now bring a claim for this sort of breach of contract in the employment tribunal following a case brought by an applicant whose offer of employment was withdrawn by the employer (*Sarker* v. *South Tees Acute Hospitals NHS Trust*).

Medical Testing

Do you Have to Agree to a Medical Examination?

Employers sometimes make an offer of employment dependent on passing a medical examination. This begs an obvious question – do you have to agree to undergo the test? Usually the answer will be quite simple – no medical examination, no job. However, if you are the only person required to undergo the test, then you may well have a discrimination claim. For instance, if you are disabled and the employer cannot justify making you have a test, then he or she will probably be guilty of discrimination if you were the only applicant required to take it.

What Happens if you Fail the Medical?

If you fail the medical, the conditional offer is likely to be withdrawn. This will not constitute a breach of contract because the offer was conditional on the medical but, depending on the circumstances, you may want to consider a discrimination claim (see below).

Can you Claim Negligence?

What if the doctor was negligent in the way he or she carried out the medical?

Unfortunately, the Court of Appeal has said that negligence claims cannot be brought by prospective employees against medical practitioners retained by employers in respect of pre-employment medical examinations (*Kapfunde* v. *Abbey National plc*). Amazingly this was held to be the case even if the doctor's negligent assessment led to the offer of employment being withdrawn. The same applies to advice given on the basis of a medical questionnaire.

However, the applicant in the above negligence claim might have been able to bring a claim for racial discrimination because the refusal to employ her was on the basis of her sickle cell status, the rationale being that she was likely to require a lot of time off work. Equally, she might have been able to run a disability claim challenging the employer's assumptions. For instance, the Code of Practice to the Disability Discrimination Act says that medical evidence about a disability will not usually justify an adverse employment decision (although clearly it can do) if it has no substantial effect on the person's ability to do the job.

2
Getting Started

Now that you've got over the first hurdle of finding a job, you need to establish your employment status – in other words, you need to figure out whether you are an employee or not. You may think it obvious – and it will be if you have a contract of employment – but otherwise, it may not. For instance, the employment status of casual workers, contract workers, bank nurses, homeworkers or those working for an agency is often difficult to ascertain.

The distinction is important because generally it is only *employees* who can benefit from statutory employment rights, such as the right to claim unfair dismissal (see Chapter 6). Some statutory health and safety protection also depends on employee status. In addition, if you are self-employed, employers do not usually pay your tax and national insurance, provide holiday pay, sick pay or pension benefits. Only employees will have a contract of employment, so it is important to establish what it is and what you can expect to find in it.

The Contract of Employment

What is it?
Basically, a contract is an agreement entered into by two parties, giving rise to obligations which are recognised or enforced by the law. Until a woman accepts the offer of a job, there is no contract between the offerer (the employer) and the offeree (the woman). None of the stages leading up to that point – advertisement, application or interview – bind either of the parties into a legal framework.

However, once she has accepted the offer made by the employer, the woman becomes bound by the terms of that offer. It is important to note that a contract need not be in writing (although it helps in order to establish the terms agreed) in order to be legally binding. An employee does, however, have the right to demand a written statement of the terms of her employment (see below for more details).

What are the Express Terms of the Contract?

These are the terms agreed explicitly between the parties, usually in writing, although they do not have to be in order to be legally binding.

Under section 1 of the Employment Rights Act (ERA) 1996, the employer is required to provide a written statement within two months of the employee's starting date, which must contain the following terms:

- Name of the employee
- Name of the employer
- Starting date
- Date that continuous employment began
- Job description/title
- Remuneration and intervals at which it is paid
- Hours of work
- Holiday entitlement and pay
- Sickness entitlement and pay
- Pensions and pension scheme
- Period of employment or date of fixed term, if not permanent
- Place of work or locations if more than one and the employer's address
- Details of collective agreements applicable to the employment
- Details of disciplinary and grievance procedures
- Notice details

If the employer agrees any changes with the employee to the contract of employment, he or she must also put these in writing within one month of the changes being made (section 4 of the ERA 1996).

What are the Implied Terms of the Contract?

Although not expressly written or stated in the contract of employment, implied terms are terms which become part of the contract and which place obligations on the parties just as binding as express terms. However, implied terms cannot contradict express terms and almost never take precedence over them if there is a conflict between the two.

What are the Implied Terms which Place Obligations on the Employer?

The implied terms that an employer has to observe include the following:

- A duty to maintain a relationship of mutual trust and confidence
- A duty to pay the employee
- A duty to care for the health and safety of the employee:

  In one case (*Johnstone* v. *Bloomsbury Health Authority*), the Court of Appeal held that the employers of a junior hospital doctor could not lawfully require him to work so much overtime in one week as to damage his health.

- A duty to provide a safe system of work
- A duty to provide a safe working environment
- A duty to provide proper and suitable equipment and keep it in a safe condition
- A duty to reimburse authorised expenses
- A duty to select reasonably fit and competent fellow employees
- A duty to provide a grievance procedure:

  This is a fairly recent development (*LA Goold (Pearmak) Ltd* v. *McConnell and anor*). The Employment Appeal Tribunal said that there was an implied term in the contract of employment that employers should respond promptly to employees' grievances.

- A duty to provide a suitable working environment:

  In one case (*Waltons and Morse* v. *Dorrington*), an employer failed to ban smoking in a poorly ventilated workplace, after it became clear that measures already introduced to resolve the problem of passive smoking were inadequate.

What are the Implied Terms which Place Obligations on the Employee?

The implied terms that an employee has to observe include the following:

- A duty to serve in person – that is, do the work yourself
- A duty to keep secrets and not to disclose confidential information obtained in the course of employment
- A duty to act in good faith
- A duty to obey reasonable and lawful instructions
- An obligation to perform duties with reasonable care and skill
- A duty to render honest and faithful service
- A duty not to be absent from work without good cause
- A duty to take reasonable care of her health and safety and that of others

Is Custom and Practice an Implied Term?

A term may become implied into an employment contract if it is used regularly. Basically, both parties need to be aware of it and to agree tacitly that it has become a contractual term although it has never been put into writing.

To establish that a custom has become a contractual term, it must be 'reasonable, notorious and certain' (*Sagar* v. *H Ridehalgh & Son Ltd*). That means it must be fair and not arbitrary or capricious; it must be established and well known; and it must be clear-cut. However, trying to establish that a term has become established in this way is usually a last resort.

A single incident is not enough to establish that an implied term has become part of the contract by custom and practice. But if it goes on for a long period of time and is recognised by both parties to have become the established custom, then it is likely to have become an implied, contractual term.

What about Terms which Become Incorporated?

Incorporation means that certain terms have become implied as part of the contract. Parties can agree to incorporate terms into employment contracts from a variety of sources, such as collective agreements, works rules and disciplinary codes.

Incorporation may be express, that is, the individual employment contract states that certain of its terms are regulated by a collective agreement. Or it may be implied, such as when there is a clear and established custom that terms of collective agreements are incorporated into individual contracts and it is obvious that the parties would have agreed to this when the contract was instituted.

Policies can also become incorporated. In one case (*Taylor* v. *Secretary of State for Scotland*), the House of Lords found that the terms of the Scottish Prison Service's equal opportunities policy had been incorporated into the applicant's contract of employment.

Are there any Terms which are Imposed by Legislation?

A number of terms in contracts are imposed by statute, as well as a wide range of employment protection rights. Any attempt to contract out of any of these by an employer will be void. They include:

- Equal Pay Act 1970
- Health & Safety At Work Act 1974
- Race Relations Act 1976
- Sex Discrimination Act 1975
- Disability Discrimination Act 1995
- Employment Rights Act 1996
- Trade Union and Labour Relations (Consolidation) Act 1992
- Transfer of Undertakings (Protection of Employment) Regulations 1981

Employment Status

Are you an Employee or Not?

There is no *comprehensive* legal test of what constitutes an employee, a worker (for instance, someone who works on a casual basis) or a self-employed person (for instance, someone who runs their own business), mainly because the courts have said that each case has to be considered separately. As a result, the courts have had to construct a series of tests to help figure out someone's employment status.

The following lists, based on those criteria, should help you decide whether you are an employee or not.

You are likely to be an employee if most of the following apply:

- You are required to turn up for work in person to do the job
- You are paid a regular wage or salary
- The employer makes deductions at source for tax and national insurance
- The employer pays you sick pay, holiday pay and pension benefits
- The employer is required to provide you with work and you are obliged to accept it (known as 'mutuality of obligation')
- The employer has a degree of control over the work that you do and how you do it
- The employer can hire and fire you
- The employer has the power to fix the hours you work
- You are highly integrated into the employer's organisation
- The employer provides the equipment you use
- The employer provides you with a uniform that you are required to wear

On the other hand, a court is likely to decide that you are not an employee if:

- You are not required to do the work personally
- You can determine the hours you work
- You provide your own equipment, tools and premises
- You hire your own helpers
- You control the way in which the work is carried out
- You have the right to set the rate charged
- You pay tax and national insurance on a 'self-employed' basis
- You are registered for VAT
- You can carry out work for others at the same time as working for a particular employer

How do the Courts Apply the Tests?

Remember that the above are only the indicators of a person's employment status. Given that the facts of a situation will be different in every case, the courts will often come to different conclusions although the circumstances appear to be the same.

For instance, in one case (*Sreekanta* v. *Medical Relief Agency (Stoke on Trent) Ltd*) a doctor working part time for a medical relief agency was found to be self-employed, because he had a large degree of control over what he did and he did not have to do the work himself.

By contrast, in another case (*Narich Proprietary Ltd* v. *Commissioner of Pay-Roll Tax*), some lecturers in weight-watching classes who could also use substitutes for their work were deemed to be employees because of the high degree of control exerted by the company over how they should teach.

But control will not always be the determining factor, if all the other factors point to a different conclusion.

Take the case of the sub-postmaster (*Hitchcock* v. *Post Office*) who provided his own premises, equipment and assistants. He carried all the financial risk and could delegate his functions. He was deemed to be self-employed despite the fact that the Post Office exercised a lot of control over how he ran his business.

What about the Employment Status of Homeworkers and Casual Workers?

There is no statute dealing with the employment status of home-workers or casual workers, with the exception of the National Minimum Wage Act which defines a homeworker as someone who contracts to work for someone's business, but who is not under their management or control. Instead, the law has developed on the basis of individual cases. Unfortunately, the courts have put great emphasis on the 'mutuality of obligation' criterion – bad news for casual workers and homeworkers who are almost never required to accept or reject work.

For instance, in a well-known case (*O'Kelly* v. *Trusthouse Forte*), the Court of Appeal said that there could only be a contract of employment if a worker was obliged to accept work and the employer obliged to provide it. Otherwise, the arrangement amounted to no more than a series of daily contracts. As a result, it has been difficult for these workers to establish employee status.

This approach was confirmed in a recent case (*Carmichael* v. *National Power plc*), when the House of Lords said that two women who were employed as guides in a power station on a casual basis were not employees because there was no mutuality of obligation between the parties.

On a more positive note, the provisions of the discrimination legislation are helpful to homeworkers. Under the Equal Pay Act, the Sex Discrimination Act, the Race Relations Act and the Disability Discrimination Act, the concept of employment is extended to include workers and the genuinely self-employed.

For instance, only employees are covered by the maternity provisions of the Employment Rights Act, but in one recent case (*Caruana* v. *Manchester Airport plc*) a self-employed researcher who was sacked when she announced that she was pregnant was successful in her claim of direct sex discrimination under the Sex Discrimination Act. She could not bring a claim under the Employment Rights Act because she was not an employee.

What is a Fixed-term Contract?

A fixed-term contract is a contract that has a definite termination date, even if you or the employer can give notice to end it before the specified date. If there is no notice period, then you have a contract that effectively guarantees employment for the fixed term. For instance, if you have a contract that says you will be employed from January 2001 to December 2004 and the contact is terminated in December 2002, then you are entitled to payment for two more years, as long as there is no notice period in the contract.

What Rights do you Have under a Fixed-term Contract?

As an employee on a fixed-term contract (and you will be an employee if you have a fixed-term contract of employment) you have the same employment rights as someone on a permanent contract if you are dismissed before it comes to an end. So not only can you bring a claim for unfair dismissal or unfair selection for redundancy (as long as you have the required length of service and have not opted out of your statutory rights), but you can also bring a discrimination claim. For instance, if your contract is not renewed at the end of the fixed term, you can claim unfair dismissal.

Can you Waive your Right to Bring an Unfair Dismissal Claim under a Fixed-term Contract?

Until recently employees on fixed-term contracts of one year or more could agree with an employer to forfeit the right to bring a claim for unfair dismissal when the contract ended. The advantage to the employer of these waiver clauses was clear – the chance to avoid unfair dismissal claims once the fixed-term contract period was up.

However, the law has changed recently so that employees on fixed-term contracts issued or extended after 25 October 1999 can no longer opt out of their statutory right to bring a claim for unfair dismissal. (But note that employees with contracts of two years or more can still opt out of their statutory redundancy rights.) So even if your employer invites you to sign such a clause and you do so, it will no longer have any validity in law.

What does the European Directive on Fixed-term Workers Say?

Although fixed-term workers enjoy all the same statutory employment rights as their permanent counterparts, they clearly do not enjoy the same security of employment. As a result, the European Commission recently adopted a directive to strengthen the position of fixed-term workers. The directive, which applies only to employees, states that a fixed term is a contract or relationship limited by reference to an end date, the completion of a task or the happening of a specific event.

The directive introduces two principles for fixed-term workers:

- Non-discrimination. That means that member states of the European Union have to introduce legislation into their own country to ensure that fixed-term workers are not treated less favourably than permanent staff, unless it can be justified
- Preventing abuse. To stop employers from abusing a succession of fixed-term contracts to avoid giving someone permanent status, member states have to introduce one of the following measures:
  1. objective reasons justifying the renewal of fixed-term contracts

2. an agreed maximum for the length of time that successive fixed-term contracts can last
3. a limit to the number of renewals

The directive will take effect in July 2001 and the UK must amend its laws to bring them into line with the directive by then.

What are Zero Hours' Contracts?

Under the terms of a zero hours' contract, you are contracted to work for an organisation with no guarantee of minimum working hours or earnings. The employer requires you to be completely flexible, to turn up for work often at very short notice but with no guarantee of the number of hours you might be required to work that week.

What is the Status of Someone on a Zero Hours' Contract?

Workers on zero hours' contracts may not even be able to establish that they are employees. If the arrangements are very imprecise, the employer may be able to argue that the worker is free to refuse any work offered and that the employer is not under an obligation to offer work (see section on casual workers). The fact that refusal would result in the worker not being offered work again in the future does not seem to have cut much ice with the courts so far.

Do you Have the Right to Be Paid for the Hours you Have Worked?

In the past, some zero hours' workers were not even paid for the time spent at work, only for the time spent working. This practice has now been outlawed by the provisions of the National Minimum Wage Act 1998 which state that workers must be paid for the hours when they are at work and available for work (excluding rest breaks).

Can your Employer Include a Probationary Period Clause in the Contract?

Although there is nothing you can do to stop your employer from inserting a probationary period into your contract (unless you are very senior and can dictate terms), make sure that you clarify the grounds on which your contract could be terminated because of poor performance. Put this in writing once the criteria have been agreed. If there are subsequent problems which have nothing to do with the criteria you established with the employer, then you may well have a case to pursue for breach of contract.

Employment of Women from Overseas

Until recently, there were no sanctions for an employer hiring people whom they knew to be in breach of their immigration status. However, under section 8 of the Asylum and Immigration Act 1996, it is now a criminal offence for an employer to hire someone who is not allowed to work in this country.

Whom does the Asylum and Immigration Act Apply to?

The Asylum and Immigration Act applies to anyone who started work after 27 January 1996. Employers are not, therefore, required to make checks on employees who started before that date. You can challenge any employer who does so under the Race Relations Act. The maximum fine under section 8 is £5,000, but there is no limit on compensation for unlawful race discrimination.

The Act does not apply to:

- British citizens
- Irish citizens
- Commonwealth citizens (with the right to live in the UK)
- Citizens from the European Union
- Anyone subject to immigration control (as long as her permission to be in the UK has not expired and that it allows her to work)
- Asylum seekers who are allowed to work
- Anyone allowed to work under the Immigration Rules
- People who had previously been allowed to work waiting for the outcome of an appeal

What does the Act Require the Employer to Do?

The employer has to ask a prospective employee (that is, someone working under a contract of employment or an apprenticeship contract) for one of a number of documents to verify her work status before taking her on. These could include any of the following:

- Passport
- Certificate of registration

- Birth certificate
- National identity card
- Work permit
- Document stating her National Insurance number, such as a P45 or a pay slip

The employer then has to check the document and decide whether it looks valid or not, although he or she is not required to investigate its authenticity. Having done all that, the employer then has to keep a record of the document.

In its guide for employers on the Asylum and Immigration Act, the Commission for Racial Equality explains that the Act does not require employers to find out whether employing a particular individual would be legal. Unless the employer knows that employing the woman would be illegal, he or she just has to have a look at one of the documents and satisfy him or herself that it looks valid.

How does the Employer Know Whom to Ask?

This is a crucial question. The Commission for Racial Equality and the Home Office both recommend that any questions about work permits should be asked of all applicants, otherwise the employer may end up being accused of unlawful racial discrimination.

If you suspect that you are the only person to have been asked for documentation to verify your work status, you may well have a claim for discrimination. Proving that you were the only one asked may, however, be a different matter. Have a look at Chapter 1 for a more detailed explanation of the obligations of employers to job applicants under the Race Relations Act and for the sort of documents you can ask the employer to disclose to you to back up your claim.

What Should you do if you are Asked to Produce a Document?

If you are asked to produce a document, the Commission for Racial Equality recommends that you ask your employer for time to do so. It states that if you can satisfy the employer that you will be able to produce the required document within a reasonable time while other aspects of the appointment are finalised, the employer should consider postponing the vacancy until you can produce it. Failure to do so may constitute unlawful racial discrimination. The employer might also be guilty of discrimination if he or she rejected you because he or she could not read or could not understand the document you produced. However, if you fail to produce any evidence about your work status, then you are unlikely to succeed in your claim.

For instance, in one of the few cases decided under the Act (*Caulker* v. *Bluebird Foodmarket and ors*), a tribunal held that an employee was not discriminated against when he did not produce any of the appropriate paperwork showing he had the right to work here.

3
Equality in the Workplace

Now that you are established in the workplace, don't assume that you will automatically be treated in the same way as your male counterparts in terms of pay and other conditions. Despite nearly a quarter of a century of equal pay legislation, full-time women workers earned only 80 per cent of full-time men's hourly pay in 1998, while part-time women earned less than 60 per cent. This pay gap is one of the widest in Europe.

And don't think that it applies only in jobs where men and women tend to be segregated, such as nursing or cleaning. It applies within professions where men and women are equally represented. For instance, although more women than men have been qualifying as solicitors over the last few years, the Law Society's annual survey in 1999 revealed that the average earnings of women solicitors was still falling short of men at all levels.

Although we have come a long way from the Factory and Workshop Act 1891 which forced employers to expel women from the workforce when they became pregnant and gave them no right of return, women are still being dismissed for becoming pregnant in 2000. True, they can now bring a claim of sex discrimination or unfair dismissal, but the end result is that they still end up without a job, albeit with some compensation if they succeed in their claim.

It is a sad fact of life that women are still being discriminated against in the workplace. You need to know your rights if you are going to do something about it.

Equal Pay

What is the Relevant Legislation?

The relevant UK law on equal pay is contained in:

• The Equal Pay Act 1970 which covers *all* contractual terms, not just those dealing with pay. (The Sex Discrimination Act only covers claims dealing with non-contractual issues, such as allocation of work, access to promotion, training and transfers)
• The Pensions Act 1995

The relevant EC measures are contained in:

• Article 141 of the Treaty of Amsterdam (previously Article 119 of the Treaty of Rome) which establishes the principle that women and men should get equal pay for work of equal value
• Equal Pay Directive 1975 which says that men and women should be treated the same in all aspects of remuneration for the same work

What is the EOC Code of Practice?

The Equal Opportunities Commission has produced a Code of Practice which, although not legally binding, can be used in evidence before an employment tribunal. The Code recommends that employers review their pay·systems for sex bias by way of a detailed eight-stage process as follows:

• By undertaking a thorough analysis of the pay system to produce a breakdown of all employees by sex, job title, grade, whether part-time or full-time along with all details of their remuneration
• By examining each element of the pay system against the above data
• By identifying any elements of the system which the review indicates may be the source of discrimination
• By changing any rules or practices which the analysis has identified as giving rise to discrimination
• By analysing the likely effects of any proposed changes to the pay system before implementation
• By giving equal pay to current employees

- By setting up a system of regular monitoring
- By drawing up and publishing an equal pay policy

The Code can be obtained free of charge from the Commission (see Chapter 8 for address).

How does the Equal Pay Act Work?

The Equal Pay Act says that every contract of employment has an implied term that men and women should be paid the same. This means that where a woman can show that she is employed on

- Work which is the same or broadly similar, known as 'like work', or
- Work which is rated equal under a job evaluation scheme, or
- Work which is of equal value

with a man in the 'same employment', then providing the employer cannot justify the difference, her contract will be modified to be no less favourable than his.

Who Can You Have as Your Comparator?

To make a claim, you have to compare yourself with someone who has (or has had) the same employer as you.

That can include someone in the 'same establishment or service' (*Scullard* v. *Knowles*). But it does not include employees of an undertaking that has been contracted out from the public to the private sector (*Lawrence and ors* v. *Regent Office Care Ltd and ors*). In *Allonby* v. *Accrington and Rossendale College and ors*, the appeal tribunal said that a man employed by a college could not be compared with a woman supplied by an agency to the college.

The woman can also make a comparison with her successor (*Diocese of Hallam Trustee* v. *Connaughton*) or predecessor (*Macarthys Ltd* v. *Smith*) as well as someone who is currently employed.

It is up to the claimant to choose the comparator (as long as he is a man), not the tribunal or the employer. The employer cannot stop a woman bringing a claim for equal value with a man even if there is another man doing the same work as her. If she wants, a woman can compare her job with a number of men, or a class of comparator, although the tribunal might choose the most relevant men out of that class.

And if the woman is having problems choosing a comparator, she can ask for documents to be disclosed (a process known as disclosure) to help her identify someone appropriate. Or she can use a sex discrimination questionnaire (see Chapter 7) to elicit information from her employers about the identity of potential comparators.

Who is Entitled to Claim and what Can Be Claimed?

Anybody in employment can claim whatever their age, length of service or gender. In addition, the Act applies to homeworkers, the self-employed, contract workers and apprentices.

Equal pay covers any financial terms and conditions of employment governed by the contract of employment and any collective agreements. This includes basic pay, bonus pay, payment by results, sick pay benefits, redundancy payments (contractual and statutory), unfair dismissal compensation, holidays, shift and overtime premiums, pension benefits and access to membership of pension schemes, as well as benefits such as company cars and luncheon vouchers.

How Long Can you Backdate your Claim for?

If you are successful in your claim and are awarded back pay, this is no longer limited to a maximum of two years from the date you lodged your claim at the employment tribunal, following a recent ruling by the European Court of Justice (*Levez* v. *TH Jennings (Harlow Pools)*). You should therefore claim back pay for every year of underpayment, although it may be limited to six years.

What does the Concept of 'Like Work' Mean?

The law says that a woman is employed on like work if she does the same, or broadly similar, work to that of her comparator and there are no differences of any practical importance between what they do.

There are three stages in a 'like work' claim:

• First of all, you have to show that your work is the same or broadly similar to that of your male comparator. The courts have said that the question of whether two jobs are broadly similar can be answered by a general consideration of the type of work involved and the skills and knowledge required to do them. It is not necessary to undertake a minute examination of the differences between the two jobs

- Then the tribunal has to decide whether there are any differences between the two jobs which are of practical importance. When comparing differences, the tribunal will consider: how many differences there are; the kinds of differences that exist; the extent of the differences; and how frequently the differences occur. There are no hard and fast rules about what constitutes a difference of practical importance between the two jobs. Each case will be decided on its own merit, but the courts have said that trivial differences will not rule out an equal pay claim

- Finally, the employer can defend the difference in pay if he or she can show that there is a material factor (sometimes known as a material difference) which explains the pay gap between the job holders (see below), but has nothing to do with the difference in sex between them

What does the Concept of 'Work Rated as Equivalent' Mean?

The second way open to a woman to claim equal pay under the Act is to show that she is employed on work which has been rated as equivalent to that of a man under a job evaluation study (JES). An employer is not under a legal obligation to conduct a JES, but once he or she does so and the results are accepted, the woman is entitled to rely on it to gain equal pay, even if it is never implemented.

A woman will be regarded as being employed on work rated as equivalent if one of the following situations applies:

- If a job evaluation study shows that the jobs have equal value
- *Or* – and this is important – the jobs would have been given equal value if the evaluation study itself had not been flawed

That means that an employer cannot get round an equal pay claim by relying on a JES which is, in itself, discriminatory. Conversely, however, if the JES cannot be shown to be tainted, the woman has little or no chance of succeeding with an equal pay claim. Indeed, tribunals are not allowed to consider an equal *value* claim if a non-discriminatory JES has found that the work of the claimant and her comparator are unequal.

What is an Analytical JES?

The courts have said that an evaluation scheme has to be *analytical* in order to be valid. An analytical JES must observe the following rules:

- The jobs of each worker covered by the study must have been valued in terms of the demands made on the workers under various headings such as skill, effort and decision-making
- Comparisons on a 'whole job' basis (with jobs being assessed in terms of their overall content) is not enough, mainly because such comparisons do not analyse why one order of job ranking is fairer than another. This is because the 'whole job' (or non-analytical) approach can reinforce traditional views about the value of women's jobs in comparison to those of men

If you want to challenge an analytical JES which has included your job, you should use your employer's internal appeals procedure in the first instance and get the help of your union, if you are a member of one. It will be up to you to show that there is a fundamental error in the scheme such as the failure to include a factor which is an important element in your job, or if the JES is inaccurate or very out of date.

Is your Case Scuppered if you Score Less Points than a Man under a JES?

Even if, under a JES, you score a different number of points to a man, you may still be entitled to claim that you are employed on work rated as equivalent.

> For instance, in one case (*Springboard Sunderland Trust* v. *Robson*), a woman scored 410 points and the man scored 428, putting both of them in the same salary grade. The Employment Appeal Tribunal said that where the job evaluation process involves translating points into a salary grade, then it is the *final grade* which determines whether the jobs are rated as equivalent.

What does the Concept of 'Equal Value' Mean?

When a woman brings an equal value claim, what she is saying to her employer is that the demands of her work should be given the same value as her male comparator, although the two jobs may be completely different. Unfortunately, these cases have proved horrendously complex and some have taken years to resolve. That being so, you should bring a claim for 'like work' at the same time as your equal value claim as these tend to be more straightforward. The tribunal will hear the 'like work' claim first, and it is only if that fails that the case will proceed down the equal value route.

Incidentally, the House of Lords have said (*Pickstone* v. *Freemans plc*) that your claim for equal *value* with a man will not be barred just because there is a different man doing the same job as you, and who is paid the same as you. In other words, even if there is a man doing 'like work' to you, you can still bring an equal value claim with someone else as your comparator.

What Procedure do you Have to Follow in an Equal Value Claim?

There is a particular procedure which equal value claims have to follow:

- The tribunal will hold an initial hearing to decide whether your case has any hope of success. The employer can try to block the claim at this stage by showing that the job in question is covered by a valid job evaluation study, or by arguing that there is a good reason for the variation in pay (known as a genuine material factor)
- If your claim passes this initial test, then the tribunal will decide whether to appoint an independent expert to prepare a report on whether the jobs are of equal value. If the tribunal decides not to, it still has to offer you the chance to appoint your own expert
- Alternatively, the tribunal can bypass this stage and go to a full hearing to consider the issue for itself. If the matter is referred to an expert, the tribunal considers his or her report at a full hearing. If the tribunal resolves the issue in your favour, employers can raise the material factor defence at this stage, although if they already raised this argument unsuccessfully at the initial hearing, then they will not usually be allowed another bite at the cherry

What is a Material Factor Defence?

If a woman can show that she is engaged in 'like work', 'work rated as equivalent', or 'work of equal value', then the tribunal will presume that the difference between her salary and that of the man is due to the fact that she is a woman. That is, unless the employer can show that the difference has nothing to do with her sex – this is known as the material factor defence.

What does the Employer Have to Prove?

There are three distinct elements to the defence that the employer has to prove:

* First of all, the employer has to show that the difference in pay is *genuinely* due to a factor which has nothing to do with the woman's sex
* Secondly, the employer has to show that the factor constitutes a material difference between the man's and the woman's case, in other words, that it is significant and relevant
* That the factor is not in itself discriminatory

  For instance, one claim (*Rainey* v. *Greater Glasgow Health Board*) succeeded on the basis that external factors, such as market forces, constituted a defence in all three types of equal pay claims. However, although this case succeeded, tribunals tend to look closely at the market forces argument to make sure that the employer is not using it as a cover for covert discrimination.

Other factors which have been accepted as a defence include:

* 'Red circling' (for example, when jobs are re-graded and the employee is allowed to remain on the higher pay grade), although not on an indefinite basis
* Geographical differences such as the payment of London Weighting
* Different skill levels and qualifications as long as they are relevant to the job in question

When does the Employer Have to Justify Objectively the Difference in Pay?

Finally, in certain circumstances where the unequal pay affects substantially more women than men (known as indirect discrimination), case law shows that the employer also has to justify objectively the different treatment as well as show that there is a material factor explaining the difference in pay.

In these circumstances, the employer has to show that the difference in treatment:

- Corresponds to a real business need on the part of the organisation; and
- Is appropriate to achieve that objective; and
- Is necessary to achieve that need

For instance, in one very long and tortuous case (*Enderby and ors v. Frenchay Health Authority and ors*), the European Court of Justice said that where statistics show a significant difference in pay between two jobs of equal value, one of which is dominated by women and the other by men, the employer has to show that the difference was based on factors which could be objectively justified and which were unrelated to any sex discrimination. In this instance, the court decided that the fact that the respective rates of pay were arrived at by separate collective bargaining procedures was irrelevant.

The Spanish Women's Institute has produced a useful checklist aimed at pinpointing wage discrimination and discrimination in job evaluation. For details see Equal Opportunities Review 86, July/August 1999.

Discrimination in Pay Systems

All pay systems have potentially discriminatory features. This could be due to lack of equality of access to particular benefits for women or because women do not have equal access to all the elements of the pay system.

What about Seniority and Service-related Benefits?

These may operate against women because of breaks in service due to having children. Get your employer to check that all periods of employment are included when assessing eligibility for service-related benefits, particularly absences on maternity leave.

What about Bonuses and Performance-related Pay?

It is important to check that bonus payments and productivity pay are not used by employers as a way of maintaining differentials between different groups of workers who are segregated on gender grounds. For instance, local authority wet weather bonuses are given to groundsmen whatever the weather, but are not available for traditionally female jobs.

If women are on maternity leave when bonuses and performance-related payments are made, it is important to make sure that these are reflected in their maternity pay. The employer is probably entitled to reduce the payment proportionately to reflect the amount of time taken off for maternity leave, but only if it is relevant to the time when the calculation is made. For instance, if a bonus is given in December for work done in the first six months of the year and the woman starts her leave in November, she should receive the full amount.

In a recent case heard by the European Court of Justice (*Lewen* v. *Denda*), the court said that it was not discriminatory to refuse to pay a Christmas bonus to a female worker on parental leave where the sole condition for payment of the bonus was that the employee was in active employment at the time it was awarded. The court added, however, that where the bonus is paid retrospectively for work done during the year, the employer must pay a sum proportionate to the amount of time that the employee has worked during the year. There seems no reason why the same logic should not apply to maternity leave.

What about Overtime and Shift Premiums?

Unfortunately, the courts have stated that it is not discriminatory against women for employers to refuse to pay overtime rates until they have exceeded the number of hours for full-time work. In other words, if a woman works, say, 21 hours per week but the full-time hours are 35, she cannot trigger an overtime payment until she has worked 35 hours

Maternity Rights

What Statutory Protection is there?

The Employment Rights Act 1996 gives specific rights to pregnant women and women on maternity leave protecting them against unfair dismissal and redundancy, as well as the right to return to their jobs. But to benefit from these rights you have to be an employee (see Chapter 2).

As a result of recent changes to the law, employees have been given an additional right – that they should not be subjected to detrimental treatment because they were pregnant, had given birth or had taken maternity leave. Previously there was no such right under the Employment Rights Act and women had to claim discrimination under the Sex Discrimination Act.

However, if you are not an employee, you still have to rely on the Sex Discrimination Act (which covers workers and the self-employed as well as employees) although it makes no explicit reference to pregnancy or maternity leave. You can use the Act to make a claim of sex discrimination, but only during the period of your pregnancy and/or maternity leave.

What Maternity Rights do Women Have?

All women, irrespective of length of service or hours of work, are now entitled to 18 weeks' unpaid maternity leave from their employer. During this period, they retain *all* their contractual rights, apart from the right to be paid (see later under statutory maternity pay). At least two weeks must be taken by the woman around the time of the birth. Any employer who contravenes this provision will be guilty of a criminal offence.

What does a Woman Have to Tell her Employer and When?

In order to apply for maternity leave, a woman must give her employer the following information (not necessarily in writing) at least 21 days before she intends to stop work:

- That she is pregnant
- The date when the baby is due
- The date when her maternity leave is due to start, in writing if the employer requests it
- That she wants statutory maternity pay (if eligible)

If the employer asks for a certificate giving the expected date of birth, the woman must provide it – usually a form called a MAT B1, which is obtainable from a midwife or doctor.

In terms of returning to work:

- A woman does not have to tell her employer that she intends to return to work
- If she wants to return before the end of the 18 weeks, she has to give 21 days' notice, in writing.
- A woman returning at the end of the 18-week period has the right to return to the *same* job with all the same terms and conditions
- If she is too ill to return, the normal sick leave procedures apply

Remember if you decide not to return to work, you have to give your employer the notice period stipulated in your contract of employment.

When Can a Woman Start her Maternity Leave?

Usually the woman can choose when to start her leave, as long as it is not before the eleventh week before the baby is due. However, if the woman is off work with a pregnancy-related illness in the six weeks before it is due, the employer can trigger the maternity leave. Giving birth will, not surprisingly, automatically trigger the start of the maternity leave.

What about Women with at Least One Year's Service?

Women with at least one year's service with the same employer are entitled to an additional period of maternity absence, which starts at the end of the ordinary maternity leave and ends 29 weeks after the birth. But note that you must have one year's service under your belt by the start of the eleventh week before the baby is due.

In order to apply for additional leave, a woman must notify her employer (not necessarily in writing) at least 21 days before the start of the leave:

- That she is pregnant
- The date when the baby is due (backed up by a medical certificate, if requested by the employer)
- The date when her maternity leave will start, in writing if the employer requests it

She does not have to tell her employer at this stage that she intends to take additional maternity leave nor that she intends to return to work unless the employer specifically asks her whether she intends to return or not.

When returning to work, the following provisions apply:

- The employer can write to the woman after 15 weeks of her maternity leave, asking her to confirm the expected date of birth and whether she intends to return
- The employee has to respond within 21 days of receipt of the letter
- The employer then has to tell her the last possible date by which she must return
- If the woman wants to return early from her leave, she has to give her employer 21 days' notice, in writing, of her intended return date
- If she is too ill to return, the normal sick leave procedures apply

Remember if you decide not to return to work, you have to give your employer the notice period stipulated in your contract of employment.

What Rights do Women Have on Return to Work after Additional Leave?

If you decide to return to work, you are entitled to return from additional leave to a job of a 'prescribed' kind. This means that employers will be able to offer suitable, alternative work, but only where it is not reasonably practicable to take you back in your old job. Any alternative job offered should be on terms which are no worse than those which applied when you went off on maternity leave. This right applies to all conditions, including pay, seniority and pension rights.

If the employer refuses to let you return to the same or equivalent job, this will be considered as a dismissal because you have been denied the right to return (unless, of course, it was not reasonably practicable to do so). You may be able to bring a claim of discrimination, unfair dismissal (if you have one year's service), automatically unfair dismissal (which has no service qualification) or all three.

There is, however, a small employer exemption to this provision. Basically, the legislation says that if your employer has five or less employees just before you are due to return from your additional leave and it is not reasonably practicable for your employer to offer you suitable, alternative work, then that will not constitute an automatically unfair dismissal.

What Happens if the Woman does Not Comply with the Notice Requirements?

If a woman fails to give the required notification for the start of her leave, then it will be delayed for 21 days from the date when she should have given the notification. Anyone who starts maternity leave without giving the correct notification will be treated as being on unauthorised absence.

If the woman fails to respond to the employer's request for confirmation of her date of return within the correct time limit, then the employer can instigate the disciplinary procedure. Alternatively, if she wants to return early and does not give the correct notice of 21 days to her employer, the employer can postpone her return to work for 21 days.

If the woman is unable to return on the due date because of illness, then the normal sick leave procedures will apply. She must, of course, provide a sickness certificate to the employer as soon as possible.

What Happens to Holidays during Maternity Leave?

During ordinary maternity leave, the woman continues to accrue holiday leave because she retains all her contractual rights (apart from the right to be paid, of course). Women taking additional maternity leave only have the right to accrue holiday leave under the Working Time Regulations (see Chapter 5) – unless their contracts say something different – because they do not retain all their contractual rights.

Who Has the Right to Statutory Maternity Pay?

Anyone who has worked for the same employer continuously for six months or more may be entitled to Statutory Maternity Pay (SMP). To qualify, the woman must demonstrate:

- That she is earning more than the Lower Earnings Limit (a recent decision of the Employment Appeal Tribunal said that this was not indirectly discriminatory against women)

- That she has given her employer 21 days' notice of her intention to stop work
- That she has sent her employer a copy of the Maternity Certificate
- That she is still in employment with the employer in the fifteenth week before the week in which the baby is due (the 'qualifying week')

What do you Receive under SMP?

For the first six weeks, the woman is entitled to 90 per cent of her average pay, calculated from gross earnings in the eight weeks before the qualifying week. After that, she gets a basic rate of SMP for twelve weeks.

The woman is entitled to the benefit of a pay rise awarded any time during the 15 weeks before the baby is due, as well as during the period of paid maternity leave, whether backdated or not. She should also be entitled to the benefit of a bonus payment for work done during the year, albeit on a pro rata basis proportionate to the time that the employee has worked.

> In a recent case (*Abdoulaye & ors* v. *Régie Nationale des Usines Renault SA*), the European Court of Justice said that it was not discriminatory to pay a maternity bonus to women, even if new fathers did not receive anything similar. This was because there were occupational disadvantages inherent in maternity leave which did not apply to men.

What Happens if you do Not Return to Work?

Women do not have to pay back SMP to the employer if they decide not to return to work after maternity leave. However, employers can claim back higher levels of maternity pay if there is a clause in the contract to that effect or there is a written agreement with the woman. Even if that is the case, it may still be worth trying to negotiate with the employer to waive it.

Who Has the Right to Maternity Allowance?

If you do not satisfy the qualifying conditions for SMP, you may still be entitled to Maternity Allowance which you can claim from your local Benefits Agency. This is most likely to apply to women who are currently unemployed (but were working) or those who are self-employed.

You will be entitled to a fixed rate for 18 weeks if you have paid 26 weeks of National Insurance contributions in the 66 weeks before the baby is due and have earned at least £30 per week on average. If you are unsure whether you qualify, fill in the claim form (MA1) which you can get from the Benefits Agency and send it in along with your maternity certificate which you can get from your GP or midwife.

What Happens to your Occupational Pension?

If you are lucky enough to be a member of an occupational pension scheme, your employer has to continue to make full contributions during your paid period of maternity leave, although you can reduce your own contributions.

What about a Right to Time Off for Ante-natal Care?

Every woman, irrespective of length of service or hours of work, is entitled not to be unreasonably refused paid time off for ante-natal care. This includes the right to attend relaxation and exercise classes, although if they are run during out-of-work hours, then she might be expected to attend them at those times.

What about Time Off for Fertility Treatment?

There is no statutory right to time off for fertility treatment. Women undergoing such treatment have to rely on their employer's goodwill, unless they are a member of a union which has negotiated time off for, say, IVF. Otherwise they have to use their own annual leave time to attend hospital for the treatment. If, however, you are dismissed for taking time off for fertility treatment, you may be able to bring a claim of sex discrimination on the basis that a man would not have been treated in the same way.

What General Health and Safety Rules Apply?

According to the Management of Health and Safety At Work Regulations 1992 every employer is obliged to carry out a risk assessment of the workplace (see Chapter 5 for more details). This risk assessment should identify work-related hazards, evaluate the risk and determine the preventive or protective measures needed to eliminate or control the risk.

Are there Any Health and Safety Rules for the Protection of Women?

Under new amended regulations in 1994 – the Management of Health and Safety At Work (Amendment) Regulations – the assessment must look at risks to women in the workforce who are of child-bearing age, whether pregnant or not. If there is a risk to her health posed by the workplace, then once the woman has given notice to her employer that she is pregnant, the employer has to:

• Alter her working conditions and/or her hours of work
• If that is not possible, the employer then has to offer suitable alternative work, or suspend the woman on full pay. The same applies to women who work at night

The importance of doing a risk assessment before a woman of child-bearing age becomes pregnant was considered in a recent case (*Day* v. *T Pickles Farms Ltd*), concerning a woman who worked in a sandwich shop. When she became pregnant she found that the smell of the food made her so nauseous that her doctor certified her unfit for work. She later claimed constructive dismissal and sex discrimination on the basis that her employer had not carried out a risk assessment. She argued that had he done so, she would have been suspended on full pay and would not ultimately have lost her job.

The Employment Appeal Tribunal decided that employers are required to carry out a risk assessment when they employ someone of child-bearing age and an employer's failure to fulfil those obligations may amount to sex discrimination. It said that this should have been done at the start of her employment, before she became pregnant, since that was the only way to ensure that risks were avoided before the start of a pregnancy.

What if your Employer does Not Carry Out an Adequate Assessment?

If you think that your employer has not considered a risk when he or she carried out the assessment, then you should bring that to the attention of your employer or your health and safety representative. If your employer still discounts the risk, get in touch with the local Health and Safety Executive which has published a comprehensive guide listing potential physical, biological and chemical agents which could affect new and expectant mothers.

You can also complain to an employment tribunal if your employer fails to offer suitable, alternative work which is available or if your employer does not pay your normal salary during the period of suspension. Any complaints should be made within three months of the relevant date.

You can also take action in the local county court for breach of any of the duties imposed by the regulations. But you should try to resolve the matter internally first of all, otherwise the tribunal may reduce the amount of compensation to which you would have been entitled.

Are there Any Health and Safety Rules Relating to Breastfeeding?

Employers should allow mothers suitable breaks for breastfeeding and expressing milk, either within or outside the workplace, as appropriate. The Workplace (Health, Safety and Welfare) Regulations 1992 (see Chapter 5 for more details) state that employers must provide a suitable room for pregnant women and/or nursing mothers to rest. This room should be situated near toilets and should have facilities for women to be able to lie down.

What about Dismissal/Selection for Redundancy?

It is *automatically* unfair to dismiss a woman for a reason connected with pregnancy, childbirth or maternity leave. This right applies irrespective of length of service or hours of work. Women with one year's service can also claim ordinary unfair dismissal. If a woman is dismissed when pregnant or on maternity leave, the employer must give written reasons for the dismissal. A woman can bring a claim for sex discrimination and unfair dismissal within three months of the date of the act complained of.

In addition, it is *automatically* unfair to select a woman for redundancy because she is pregnant, has given birth or has taken maternity leave. Any woman made redundant during her maternity leave is entitled to be offered any suitable, alternative work. Although employers have a general obligation to offer alternative work before dismissing employees, women on maternity leave must be given first offer of any vacancy. If the employer fails to comply, then a claim for sex discrimination and unfair dismissal should be pursued within three months of the relevant date.

Part-time Workers

Do you Have a Legal Right to Work Part Time?

Although there is no absolute legal right to demand that an employer allows a woman to work part time, she may be able to rely on one or more of the following pieces of legislation:

- Sex Discrimination Act which offers the argument of indirect discrimination (see later for an explanation). The Sex Discrimination Act also legislates against discrimination on the basis of marital status. This can be very helpful in establishing part-time rights. When obtaining information from an employer to prepare a challenge, it is important to request a breakdown of the marital status of the workforce as well as a gender breakdown
- Article 141 of the Treaty of Amsterdam to argue parity of treatment as well as the Equal Treatment and Pay Directives
- Disability Discrimination Act to establish the right to part-time work for a disabled person. Under the Act, an employer must take reasonable steps to make sure that the working arrangements do not place disabled people at a substantial disadvantage. This will include considering alternative working hours and allowing time off for treatment or rehabilitation
- Part-time Workers (Prevention of Less Favourable Treatment) Regulations 2000

In addition, an employer has to justify any refusal to allow a woman to work part time. For instance, if an employer operated a blanket ban on women returning to work part time from maternity leave, that would constitute indirect sex discrimination.

What Protection do the Part-Time Workers Regulations Provide?

The Part-Time Workers Regulations became effective in July 2000 in order to implement the EC Part-Time Workers directive. The idea behind the regulations is to:

- Establish the legal principle of equal rights for part-time workers without having to demonstrate indirect sex discrimination (as you have to do if relying on the Sex Discrimination Act, for instance)
- Provide equal access for women to pay, bonus, shift, overtime and other additional payments
- Provide equal contractual terms of service such as occupational sick and maternity pay, contractual holiday entitlement
- Provide equal benefits such as share options, staff discounts and occupational pensions, access to training

The regulations apply to part-time workers, including homeworkers, agency and contract workers.

Who Can the Part-timer Compare Herself With?

Under the regulations, a part-timer has to compare herself with a comparable full-timer who is defined as:

- Someone who works for the same employer as the part-timer under the same type of contract; and
- Someone doing the same or similar work as the part-timer; and
- Someone with a similar level of qualification, skills and experience, and
- Someone who works in the same workplace or establishment (or, if that is not applicable, someone who works elsewhere but does similar work and has similar skills, etc.)

This is a narrow definition and may cause problems for part-timers trying to find a comparable full-timer.

What are the Principles Underlying the Regulations?

The regulations establish a number of important principles, notably that:

- Part-timers should not be treated less favourably than full-timers, unless the treatment can be objectively justified by the employer
- Part-timers should receive pro rata terms and conditions

If a part-timer believes she has been treated less favourably, she can ask the employer for a written statement of reasons. This should be provided within 21 days of the request and can be used in tribunal proceedings.

What Protection do the SDA and EqPA Provide?

Apart from the European directive, UK case law has already established under the Sex Discrimination and Equal Pay Acts that it is indirectly discriminatory to treat part-timers differently in the following situations:

* Paying part-timers less than full-timers (*Jenkins* v. *Kingsgate Clothing Productions*)
* Selecting part-timers first for redundancy (*Clarke* v. *Ely (IMI) Kynoch Ltd*)
* Refusing to let a woman switch to part-time work (*Home Office* v. *Holmes*), although other cases have come to the opposite conclusion because of different circumstances
* Failing to provide part-timers with equal sick pay benefits (*Rinner-Kuhn* v. *FWW Spezial-Gebaudereiningung GmbH & Co*)
* Failing to pay part-timers the full amount for time off to attend trade union courses (*Arbeiterwholfahrt der Stadt Berlin* v. *Botel*); (*Kuratorium für Dialyse und Nierentransplantation* v. *Lewark*); (*Davies* v. *Neath Port Talbot County Borough Council*)

In a case brought by the Equal Opportunities Commission (*R* v. *Secretary of State for Employment ex parte EOC*), the court said that it was indirect sex discrimination to require part-time employees to work a longer qualifying period to establish the same employment protection rights as full-timers.

Other areas where differing treatment of part-time workers could amount to sex discrimination include the following:

* Access to training opportunities
* Unequal arrangements for overtime or time off in lieu
* Unequal entitlement to attendance allowances, location allowances and shift allowances
* Unequal entitlement to premium weekend payments and on-call payments
* Unequal entitlement to profit sharing and share option schemes

- Unequal access to promotion opportunities
- Unequal entitlement to bank holidays
- Staff discounts being available only to full-timers
- Limited access to private medical insurance or any other benefit

How do the Regulations Improve on Existing Legislation?

One of the advantages offered by the regulations over the Sex Discrimination Act is that women will no longer have to jump the 'indirect discrimination' hoop (see next section). That is, they will no longer have to prove that proportionately more women are affected by the condition or requirement than men.

The regulations guarantee pro rata rights and give workers a right *to ask* to go part time. The directive requires member states to encourage part-time working and puts the onus on employers to provide information about part-time working, as well as giving consideration to such requests; tribunals will look for evidence of that in the event of a refusal.

Whether the regulations turn out to be of much use to part-timers remains to be seen because nothing very much is *required* under them. The proposals are mainly suggestions of best practice.

What about Time Limits for Bringing a Claim?

Beware of time limits for bringing a claim, particularly if you have made repeated requests to be allowed to work part time.

> Take the case of Mrs Cast (*Cast* v. *Croydon College*). She asked to job share but was refused in March 1992. She asked again in March and May 1993, after her return from maternity leave, but was again refused. In June 1993 she resigned and lodged a claim of sex discrimination. Both the tribunal and the Employment Appeal Tribunal said that her claim should have been lodged within three months of the original refusal. Luckily, the Court of Appeal disagreed, saying that where there are repeated requests to work part time, time runs from the date of the last unsuccessful request (see Chapter 7).

For further information , see also the EOC 'Guidance to Employers on the Employment of Part-time staff', and the second report of the Education and Employment Select Committee 'Part-time Working' (HC 346–1) available from the Stationery Office, price £9.70.

Job Sharers

Another form of part-time working is job sharing, whereby two people share the responsibility of one full-time job. Workers do not have the right to demand that the employer agrees to a job share, but in the event that he or she refuses, the woman would be able to bring a claim of indirect discrimination.

Job sharers divide the pay, holidays and other benefits equally between them according to the number of hours worked. Drawing up a contract for job sharers can therefore be problematic and employers would be well advised to seek professional advice. If you want to job share, keep the following points in mind:

- Each job sharer should have her own contract of employment covering salary, increments, entitlements, superannuation, cover arrangements and the procedures which apply when one post holder leaves
- Each job sharer is entitled to pro rata terms and conditions
- The allocation of hours should be agreed between the post holders and specified in the contract
- The days to be worked by the job sharers should be specified in the contract
- A period of overlap should be agreed so that both job sharers can communicate with each other and attend team meetings, briefings, etc. and, if necessary, be specified in the contract
- Holidays should be split pro rata, with public and extra holidays divided by agreement between the job share partners

Sex and Race Discrimination

What is Direct Discrimination under the SDA and RRA?

Direct discrimination under the Sex Discrimination Act and Race Relations Act consists of two elements:

- That the employer treated the woman making the complaint less favourably
- That the employer did so either because of her sex or on racial grounds

Both Acts apply to workers as well as job applicants and employees, and there is no qualifying period before a claim can be brought.

Who does the Woman Compare herself with?

The woman does not have to compare herself to an actual man – a hypothetical one will do – but it is obviously easier if one exists. Whether the comparison is real or hypothetical, the woman has to show that the man would have been treated differently in the same (or not very different) circumstances. In other words, she has to compare like with like. It would therefore be pointless making a comparison between, say, the pay of a woman cleaner who is black and that of the managing director who is white (and, no doubt, male).

But in an interesting development, the Court of Appeal has ruled (*Sidhu* v. *Aerospace Composite Technology Ltd*) that in certain circumstances, the Race Relations Act does not require a comparator. In this case, the applicant Mr Sidhu was attacked and racially insulted by a number of white men, one of whom was a fellow employee, on a family day out organised by the employers. Mr Sidhu retaliated. The employers dismissed both Mr Sidhu and the man who had attacked him. The court said that in these circumstances – which they called 'race-specific' – there was no need for Mr Sidhu to show that a white person had been, or would have been, treated differently. The same principle would apply under the Sex Discrimination Act.

Was the Woman Treated Less Favourably because of her Sex/Race?

Once the applicant has been able to show that she has been treated less favourably than a man, she then has to satisfy the 'but for' test. In other words, she has to show that 'but for' the colour of her skin or her sex, she would not have been treated the way she was. She does not have to show that the racial (or gender) grounds were the only reason for her treatment, but they do need to be the main reason. Nor does she have to show that the employer intended to discriminate – all that counts is the fact of the discrimination, not the motivation behind it.

In a recent case (*Wakeman and ors* v. *Quick Corporation and anor*), British nationals employed by a Japanese corporation failed in their complaint of race discrimination, although they were paid less than secondees from Japan. The Court of Appeal said the difference was due to the secondment and not on the grounds of race.

The Race Relations Act also goes further than the 'but for' test, in the sense that the complainant does not have to have been discriminated against on the basis of *her* race (unlike the Sex Discrimination Act which refers to less favourable treatment on the basis of *her* sex).

For instance, in a recent case (*Weathersfield Ltd t/a Van & Truck Rentals* v. *Sargent*), the white applicant was instructed to tell black or Asian callers that there were no cars for them. She resigned and successfully claimed race discrimination because she had been less favourably treated than someone who would have been prepared to carry out the discriminatory policy, although she herself had not been discriminated against on the basis of her race.

Whom Can you Bring a Claim against?

Employers are liable for their own unlawful discriminatory acts, but will also be liable if any of their employees engage in discriminatory acts 'in the course of their employment', whether or not the employer was aware of what was going on. Thanks to a recent decision of the Court of Appeal, that responsibility on employers has now been clarified.

The case (*Jones* v. *Tower Boot Co Ltd*) concerned a young man of mixed race – Raymondo Jones – who was both physically and verbally abused and assaulted by his co-workers. Not surprisingly, he left after a month. The Court of Appeal said that the employer was liable for what the employees had done, even if their misdemeanours were so extreme as to be totally unrelated to the job that the employer had authorised them to do.

This was an important decision, because if the employers had managed to persuade the court that their employees were not acting 'in the course of employment' when they abused Mr Jones, then the whole basis of the anti-discrimination legislation would have been undermined. Employers could then argue that the more extreme the abuse, the less they were responsible for it.

Although the employer is liable for the discriminatory acts of his or her employees, you can sue the individual employee as well as the employer. There may not, however, be much point unless the employee in question has the necessary funds to pay you compensation awarded to you by the tribunal. As well as being responsible for the discriminatory acts of employees, employers are now also responsible for acts committed against his or her employees by outsiders.

Take the well-known 'Bernard Manning' case as an example (*Burton* v. *De Vere Hotels*). The Employment Appeal Tribunal held that the employer subjected his employees to racial harassment when he allowed a third party – Bernard Manning – to abuse them in circumstances over which the employer had a measure of control. And that is the key word – control.

So if, for instance, you are being harassed by a third party in a situation over which the employer has some control but does nothing, you can bring a claim against your employer. In the Manning case, the court said the manager should have withdrawn the waitresses from the dining room when it became clear that they were the butt of Mr Manning's so-called humour.

What Defences Can Employers Use?

Under the legislation, employers can try to argue that they 'took such steps as were reasonably practicable' to prevent the employees from committing the discrimination. This will vary from case to case, depending on the circumstances, but often tribunals will want to know if the employer had an equal opportunities policy, although that in itself will not be enough to escape liability.

The tribunal will ask whether:

- Management and supervisory staff were trained in how to implement the policy
- Staff had their attention drawn to it, perhaps by its inclusion in, say, the works handbook or induction manual or by putting it on the works noticeboard

- The policies make clear that failure to abide by them will be treated as a serious disciplinary offence. The larger the company, the more that will be expected of it

What is Indirect Discrimination?

To establish indirect discrimination (on grounds of sex, marital status or race), a woman has to consider four questions:

- Has the woman's employer imposed a requirement or condition?
- Is there a disproportionate impact on women?
- Has the woman suffered a disadvantage because, as a woman (SDA) or as member of that racial group (RRA), she *cannot* comply with the requirement?
- Can the employer justify the requirement or condition in terms of a real need on the part of the business which, in itself, must not be discriminatory?

The point behind the concept of indirect, as opposed to direct, discrimination, is to challenge subtle forms of discrimination which have the effect, if not the intention, of excluding women or black people from the labour market.

What Constitutes a Requirement or Condition?

The phrase 'requirement or condition' (which mean more or less the same thing) can cover any ultimatum, obligation, policy, provision, clause or stipulation applied by an employer. The courts have also said that the words should be given the widest possible meaning to help eliminate subtle, covert discriminatory practices.

To constitute indirect discrimination, the following criteria must be satisfied:

- The requirement or condition should usually be absolute, that is, something that has to be complied with. For instance, if an employer says that everyone has to start work at eight o'clock, that will represent an absolute bar to some women with childcare responsibilities from continuing in that job
- There can be more than one requirement being applied, which can include refusing or denying an employee's request, for instance, to work part-time. But the request must have been

refused by the employer for there to be a requirement. If he or she is still considering it, there has not been a refusal

- Equally, the courts will not accept that there is a requirement or condition to complain about unless it has been imposed by the employer. The possibility of it happening in the future is not enough

The following have been held to amount to a requirement or condition:

- A policy that employees should not have young children
- An obligation to work full time
- The imposition of a flexible hours clause in a contract
- A requirement to start work at eight o'clock
- A requirement to work anywhere in the UK under the terms of a contractual mobility clause

For instance, in a recent case (*Hale and Clunie* v. *Wiltshire Healthcare NHS Trust*) two nurses won their claim of indirect discrimination on the basis of their marital status, when the employer introduced new shift systems which interfered with the women's childcare responsibilities.

Whatever the requirement/s being applied to you, make the basis of your complaint clear in your application because the employer is likely to come back and ask for more details about it at a later stage. Remember that your claim has to be made within three months of the condition being applied or of the employer refusing your request, unless there is an ongoing policy in operation.

Is there a Disproportionate Impact on Women?

To succeed in your claim, you have to be able to show that the requirement or condition affects considerably

- More women than men, or
- More married women than single women, or
- More black women than white men or women

It can be difficult, however, to decide which groups need to be compared. It may be enough to look at your own workforce and compare men and women doing similar jobs.

On the other hand, the statistics in your particular workplace may not bear out your argument – for instance, if it is female dominated – in which case you may be able to rely on national labour force statistics. Some tribunals will accept these without the need for detailed statistical evidence of the workforce. If you are a job applicant, you will want to compare yourself with other applicants.

How do you Get the Information you Need?

You can ask the employer in your questionnaire (see Chapter 7) for all the information you need. For instance, you may want to know the number of female full- and part-timers as opposed to the number of males, or the number of married and unmarried women who work full time and part time. Alternatively, you can get this information through the process of discovery (see Chapter 7).

How do you Work Out the Proportions?

The following is an example of how to work out the proportion of women who can comply with the requirement as opposed to men. Remember that the pool should be made up of all those of the particular group affected by the requirement or condition. For instance, in a workforce of 1,000 where it was proposed to make part-timers redundant first, the figures are as follows:

450 women can comply with the requirement to be a full-time worker and avoid redundancy
530 women in total in the pool
divide 450 by 530 (and multiply by 100) to get the *proportion* of women who can comply – 85 per cent

450 men are full-time workers and can avoid redundancy
470 men in total in the pool
divide 450 by 470 (and multiply by 100) to get the *proportion* of men who can comply – 96 per cent

In a Northern Irish case (*McCausland* v. *Dungannon District Council*), the Court of Appeal expressed this as a formula:

$$\frac{PY}{PT} \quad \text{compared with} \quad \frac{CY}{CT}$$

where P = Protestant, C = Catholic, Y = those who can comply with the requirement, and T indicates the total number of Protestants or Catholics in the pool.

Remember that the proportion of women who can comply has to be considerably smaller, although there is no legal definition of what that means, and it is the tribunal that will decide in each case.

> For instance, in one case (*London Underground* v. *Edwards (No 2)*), although only one woman train driver could not comply with new rosters, the Court of Appeal said that 95 per cent of women (20 out of 21) who could not comply with the requirement was considerably smaller than 100 per cent of men who could comply.

In addition, the court ruled that tribunals are entitled to use their general knowledge and expertise to look outside the pool and take account of the 'common knowledge' that ten times as many women as men are single parents and have primary responsibility for child-care. It has also been accepted as common knowledge by tribunals that a higher proportion of women than men work part time and that women are more likely to be secondary earners. But unfortunately tribunals will not necessarily always come to the same conclusions, even if the facts seem similar.

> For instance, in another case (*Sanderson* v. *BAA plc*) where 74 out of 75 female security guards could comply with a requirement to work shifts, in comparison with 100 per cent of men (90 in all), the tribunal said there was no indirect discrimination. Although the lower courts are bound by the decisions of the higher courts (Employment Appeal Tribunal, Court of Appeal and House of Lords), they can get round this by 'distinguishing' the case – that is, finding something that's different in their case to the other one. And that's what the tribunal did here. It said that because there were so many more women who could comply (75 as opposed to 21 in the train drivers' case), there was no indirect discrimination.

Has the Woman Suffered a Disadvantage because she Cannot Comply with the Requirement?

The woman has to be able to show why she cannot comply *in practice*, not just that she does not want to comply with, say, the requirement to work full time. Having said that, a woman does not have to show that it is impossible to do the hours, just that it is not practicable for her. For instance, she may not be able to comply with the requirement to work full-time hours because of a lack of affordable childcare. She also has to show that she cannot comply with the requirement at the time it is applied and not at some indefinable point in the future.

The woman also has to show that she has suffered a disadvantage as a result of not being able to comply with the requirement. This could be the loss of her job, either through dismissal or because she resigned (see under constructive dismissal), having to work the full-time hours, or having to take a different, lower-paid, job in order to work part time.

Can the Employer Justify the Requirement or Condition?

If the employer can show that the requirement or condition is necessary for the business, then it will not be discriminatory, even if the woman jumps all the other hurdles successfully. Remember that this only applies in cases of indirect discrimination, not direct discrimination. Although the burden is on the employer to convince the tribunal that the requirement is justified, it is helpful if the woman can produce evidence to counter those arguments.

In a European case (*Bilka-Kaufhaus GmbH* v. *Weber von Hartz*), the ECJ held that employers can justify a discriminatory practice if they can show that:

- It can be justified on grounds other than sex
- It corresponds to a real need on the part of the employer
- It is appropriate to meet that need; and
- It is necessary to that end

Case law has established that what is required is a balancing act between the employer's need to impose the requirement and its discriminatory effect. Basically, the more discriminatory the requirement, the more difficult it will be for the employer to justify it.

What Arguments by the Employer are Likely to Succeed?

When trying to justify the practice, the employer has to back up his or her arguments with objective evidence. Generalised statements should not be accepted by the courts. For instance, the European Court of Justice has said that an argument that part-timers are not as integrated into the workforce as full-timers is a generalised statement and does not provide objective justification for their exclusion.

Some of the objective arguments put forward by employers which have proved acceptable are as follows:

• The need for close collaboration
• The need for administrative efficiency
• The need for continuity of customer liaison
• Costs and resources

However, it is a matter of fact for the tribunal to look at in every case and what may be accepted as justification in one workplace may not be justified in another. Whatever the employer's argument, make sure you have evidence to counter it, particularly if you can show that other employers have found ways around it.

How do the Victimisation Provisions Work?

The victimisation provisions in the Sex Discrimination Act and the Race Relations Act are designed to prevent women from being penalised for taking action under any of the discrimination legislation. It is worth noting that the legislation extends to third parties. For instance, it will cover a man who complains that someone else is discriminating unlawfully against a woman or a white person who says that someone else is discriminating against a black colleague.

How do the Victimisation Provisions Operate?

The claimant has to show three things:

• That she has been involved in a 'protected activity'. In other words, that she brought proceedings under the Act, that she gave evidence or information in proceedings brought by someone else, or intended to do any of those things
• That she has been treated less favourably than another employee (whether real or hypothetical) who has not made a complaint.

Less favourable treatment can take many forms, such as refusing to employ, promote or train someone, reducing their wages or imposing inferior conditions, denying certain benefits, or dismissing them

• Finally, there has to be a causal link between the protected act and the less favourable treatment. This is to protect employers who have treated an employee less favourably, not because they brought proceedings against them but, for instance, because of absenteeism or misconduct on the part of the employee

Significantly, to prove that you have been victimised you do not have to show that the employer was consciously aware that he or she was victimising you.

In a recent case (*Nagarajan* v. *London Regional Transport*), Mr Nagarajan complained that, when he applied for promotion with London Transport, he was treated less favourably than others who had not previously brought proceedings against the company. The House of Lords has said that there can still be unlawful victimisation, even if the discriminator was not consciously aware that he or she was treating the employee unfavourably.

Is Post-employment Victimisation Lawful?

The answer is no, but there is a discrepancy in the law between the Race Relations Act and the Sex Discrimination Act. Under the former, the courts have said that the applicant still has to be employed by the employer for the victimisation provisions to be effective, but it does not have to be the case under the latter.

For instance, in a recent case (*Adekeye* v. *The Post Office (No 2)*), the applicant claimed that she had been discriminated against under the Race Relations Act at an internal appeal against dismissal. But because she was not employed at the time of the act complained of, the legislation did not provide any protection.

But the Employment Appeal Tribunal has said recently (*Coote* v. *Granada Hospitality Ltd*) that the Sex Discrimination Act allows a claimant to make a complaint of victimisation about events after she had left her employment. This case concerned an employee who had brought a sex discrimination claim against her former employer who subsequently refused to provide her with a reference because she had brought proceedings against them.

It seems hard to believe that, having ruled that post-employment victimisation applies to the Sex Discrimination Act, the courts will not now apply the same reasoning to the Race Relations Act.

Do you Have to Have Direct Evidence of Discrimination to Prove your Case?

Ultimately, the onus is on the applicant to prove her case on the balance of probabilities, that is, that it is more likely than not that it happened. This applies in both direct and indirect discrimination as well as victimisation cases, the only exception being that the onus is on employers in indirect discrimination cases to justify whatever requirement or condition they have imposed.

The problem for applicants is that it can often be difficult to obtain evidence to prove discrimination. For once, the courts have been helpful and have ruled that tribunals can draw an inference of race or sex discrimination from the facts of the case, without necessarily having direct evidence of bias.

In a leading case (*Zafar* v. *Glasgow City Council*), the House of Lords said that, once the woman has produced enough evidence to convince a tribunal that there was discrimination of some kind and the employer cannot explain the behaviour, the tribunal can 'make an inference' of unlawful discrimination in certain circumstances. For instance, if an employer provides an evasive answer to a sex or race discrimination questionnaire (see Chapter 7), the tribunal can draw the inference that the employer has committed a discriminatory act if he or she cannot supply a satisfactory explanation for their answers.

Disability Discrimination

The following sections concentrate on the employment provisions of the Disability Discrimination Act. However, it is also against the Act to serve someone who is disabled – or to offer a disabled woman a service – in a way which is not as good as that being offered to others or to refuse to provide the service on different terms. The only exception is that, when the health and safety of the disabled woman or other people are in danger, it would not be against the law to refuse to provide the service. It is also against the law for anyone who sells or lets land or property (or their agents) to unreasonably discriminate against disabled women.

Just recently the Act was extended still further so that anyone providing a service to the public has to consider what adjustments they can reasonably make for disabled people. For instance, shops and restaurants might have to change their layout to accommodate wheelchair users. Larger organisations, like banks and local authorities or the NHS, might have to make more information available in large print or Braille.

What do you Have to Prove for a Disability Claim to Succeed?

There are two distinct 'stages' to a disability claim:

- First of all, a woman has to fall within the definition of a disabled person. That is, she has to show that she has a '*physical or mental impairment* which has a *substantial and long-term adverse effect* on her ability to carry out *normal day-to-day activities*'
- Secondly, she then has to show that the employer discriminated against her

Whom does the Act Apply to?

The Act applies to:

- Employers with 15 or more employees. That can include the self-employed working for an employer over a period of time, however irregularly
- Employees
- Job applicants
- Contract workers

What Constitutes a Physical or Mental Impairment?

The Act does not define what constitutes physical or mental impairment, but guidance to the Act explains that sensory impairments such as blindness and hearing loss are included. Potential physical impairments include multiple sclerosis and cerebral palsy. Tribunals have found that the following come within the meaning of the term:

- Abdominal pain
- Amputated leg
- Asthma
- Colitis
- Diabetes
- Emphysema
- Spinal injury
- Epilepsy

Guidance to the Act (which is very helpful) states that for a mental illness to be covered by the Disability Discrimination Act it must be a 'clinically well-recognised illness' by a respected body such as the World Health Organisation. The Act therefore covers mental impairments such as learning difficulties as well as illnesses such as schizophrenia and manic depression. Tribunals have found mental impairments to include ME, post-traumatic stress disorder, depression and bulimia nervosa.

What Conditions are Excluded by the Act?

The following are excluded from the remit of the Act:

- Alcoholism (although impairments arising from alcoholism such as liver damage are covered)
- A tendency to set fires
- A tendency to steal
- A tendency to physical or sexual abuse of other persons
- Exhibitionism
- Voyeurism
- Hay fever

What is Meant by a Substantial Adverse Effect?

Again, 'substantial' is not defined, but it is something which is more than minor or trivial. Factors to be taken into account when assessing the effect of an impairment include:

- The time taken by someone with an impairment to carry out normal day-to-day activities compared with someone who does not have the impairment
- The way in which those activities are carried out in comparison with someone who does not have the impairment
- The cumulative effects of the impairment – although individual effects of the impairment may be modest, taken together they may have a substantial effect on day-to-day activities
- The effect of the impairment on the individual's behaviour – a woman will not satisfy the definition if she can modify her behaviour to carry out normal day-to-day activities
- The effect of the environment – temperature, humidity, time of day – on the person's ability to carry out day-to-day activities

How Long is Long-term?

To satisfy the definition in the Act, the disability must:

- Have lasted at least twelve months, or
- Be likely to have lasted twelve months, or
- Be likely to last for the rest of the lifetime of the person concerned (even if that is less than twelve months)

What are Normal Day-to-day Activities?

The phrase – normal day-to-day activities – does not mean the activities that the person carries out (or used to) at work. It means those activities that are 'normal' for most people in their everyday lives, such as using a knife and fork, putting on the kettle, cooking, etc.

The guidance to the Act says that to decide whether something is a normal day-to-day activity, tribunals need to take account of 'how far it is normal for most people and carried out by most people on a daily or frequent and fairly regular basis'. In coming to their decision, tribunals should focus on the activities which the applicant cannot perform rather than those she can carry out.

The guidance has an exhaustive list of functions that constitute day-to-day activities. The following are likely to have an adverse impact on the woman's ability to carry out normal day-to-day activities:

- Difficulty with mobility, such as climbing stairs or travelling in a car

- Difficulty with manual dexterity, such as the inability to handle a knife or fork or to press buttons on a keyboard
- Difficulty with physical co-ordination, such as putting food into the mouth with a fork
- Inability to control continence, which would include frequent, albeit minor, leakage from the bladder
- Difficulty with lifting, carrying or otherwise moving everyday objects such as books, a kettle of water, bags of shopping or a briefcase
- Difficulty with speech, hearing or eyesight such as the inability to give clear instructions orally, but not a minor stutter, lisp or speech impediment
- Difficulty with memory or an inability to concentrate, learn or understand such as following spoken or written instructions
- Inability to assess the risk of physical danger, such as the inability to operate equipment properly

In one case (*O'Neill* v. *Symm & Co Ltd*), the EAT accepted the applicant's argument that ME affected her ability to carry out day-to-day activities, because she could not walk far without getting out of breath, she had problems maintaining her balance and got cramps as well as 'pins and needles' which made it painful for her to type or hold a pen.

What Constitutes Discrimination under the Act?

The Disability Discrimination Act is very different from the Sex Discrimination and Race Relations Acts (which are, in effect, carbon copies of one another) in that there is no such thing as indirect discrimination under the Disability Act. Instead, the legislation introduces a new concept of 'the failure to make reasonable adjustments' alongside the more established ideas of direct discrimination and victimisation. In addition, the Disability Discrimination Act also allows the concept of justification of direct discrimination which is not allowed under the Sex Discrimination Act or the Race Relations Act.

In general terms, the Act says that employers will be guilty of discrimination if:

- For a reason relating to the woman's disability, they treat her less favourably than others to whom that reason does not apply; and

- They cannot justify that treatment; and
- If they fail to make adjustments when required to do so; and
- That failure is not justified

Who do you Have to Compare yourself with?

The first part of the definition is similar to race and sex discrimination legislation when it talks about treating the disabled woman less favourably than others. The difference (again) between the Disability Discrimination Act and the other discrimination legislation is the issue of the comparator.

> However, in an important decision (*Clark* v. *TDG Ltd t/a Novacold*) the Court of Appeal has recently clarified who the disabled person should compare herself with. In this case, the applicant was dismissed following a period of sick leave due to a back injury because he could no longer function in his job. Both the tribunal and the Employment Appeal Tribunal had said that the correct comparator was someone who had been off on sick leave for the same amount of time, but for a reason that did not constitute a disability under the Act.
>
> But the Court of Appeal said that the test of 'less favourable treatment' in the Disability Discrimination Act was different to the Sex Discrimination Act and the Race Relations Act, and did not require a like for like comparison. Instead, the comparator had to be someone who, unlike Mr Clark, could carry out the main functions of the job.

In other words, the court is saying that tribunals have to do two things:

- They have to look at the *reason* for the less favourable treatment of the disabled woman, *and*
- They have to look at others to whom that *reason* does not apply

This is a much easier hurdle for the applicant to jump than those set by the lower courts. In Mr Clark's case, for instance, he just had to find someone who could carry out the main functions of their job (presumably, the vast majority of the workforce) and look to see how they had been treated. Clearly he had been treated less favourably as they were still in a job and he wasn't. In some ways, the decision of the Court of Appeal makes the whole concept of the comparator redundant, as illustrated in Mr Clark's case. The onus is then put straight on the employer to justify the treatment.

What Would Constitute a 'Substantial' Reason for Less Favourable Treatment?

Less favourable treatment can only be justified if the employer's reason is relevant to the circumstances of the case and is 'substantial' – that is, more than trivial or frivolous. Consider the example of a factory worker with a mental illness who takes time off work intermittently due to her disability, but whose sick leave is not much more than that of other employees. Her sickness absence would not, therefore, constitute a 'substantial' reason for dismissal.

What Reasonable Adjustments does an Employer Have to Make?

The Act also says that, where the disabled woman is substantially disadvantaged by, say, the arrangements made by the employer for an interview or by any of the physical features of the premises, the employer is under a duty to make reasonable adjustments to facilitate the disabled woman. This obligation also applies to existing employees.

The Act also makes clear that an employer's ignorance will be no defence to a failure to make reasonable adjustments if the employer could have been expected to know of the disability. But what is the extent of the obligation?

In a recent case (*Rideout* v. *TC Group*) an applicant with photosensitive epilepsy was interviewed in a room with lighting which she felt had put her at a disadvantage. She had mentioned the fact of her disability in advance, although she made no comment at the interview. The court said that there was a balancing act to be established between the needs of the employee (or applicant) for adjustments to be made and the extent of the obligation on the employer to make adjustments. In this case, the applicant lost her claim.

The question, of course, is what is reasonable. The Code of Practice to the Act gives some helpful guidance as to the factors which should be taken into account when trying to decide if an adjustment would be reasonable or not:

- The extent to which taking the step would address the problem – in other words, the effectiveness of the action
- The extent to which it is practicable for the employer to take the step
- The costs of the adjustment and the disruption it would cause to the employer's business
- The extent of the employer's financial and other resources
- The availability of financial or other assistance to the employer with respect to taking the step

Case law is beginning to provide guidance on the extent to which employers should make adjustments to accommodate a disabled employee.

In one recent case (*Kenny* v. *Hampshire Constabulary*) in which the disabled person had been offered a job only to have it withdrawn because the employer could not make the necessary adjustments without huge costs, the Employment Appeal Tribunal said there could not be an onus on the employer to employ a carer as well as the disabled employee. In this case, the applicant had cerebral palsy and needed a carer to help him with urinating, but the employers could not find enough volunteers and there was no outside funding available.

In an earlier case (*Hanlon* v. *University of Huddersfield*), the Employment Appeal Tribunal held that although the employer knew that the employee was disabled and had made certain adjustments, he was not under a duty to make adjustments to provide the employee with somewhere private to massage his leg because the employer did not know, and could not have known, that those adjustments needed to be made.

What if your Employer does Not Know about your Disability?

Unfortunately for the employer, he or she can still be guilty of discrimination. According to a recent case (*H J Heinz Co Ltd* v. *Kenrick*), your employer can still discriminate against you even if he or she did not know you had a disability.

But before you get too excited, the employer is very likely to be able to justify dismissing you (for instance, on the basis of your ability to do the job). Equally, he or she would not have to make any adjustments unless they knew of the disability or could not have been expected to know in the circumstances.

What Adjustments Might an Employer Have to Make?

The following are examples of adjustments an employer may have to make:

- Making adjustments to premises
- Allocating some of the disabled woman's duties to another person
- Transferring the disabled woman to fill an existing vacancy
- Altering the disabled woman's working hours
- Assigning the disabled woman to a different place of work
- Allowing the woman to be absent during working hours for rehabilitation, assessment or treatment
- Giving the disabled woman, or arranging for her to be given, training
- Acquiring or modifying equipment
- Modifying procedures for testing or assessment
- Providing a reader or interpreter
- Providing supervision

How Can an Employer Justify Discriminating against a Disabled Person?

The legislation says that discrimination by the employer or the failure to make reasonable adjustments will only be justifiable if it is 'material to the circumstances of the case and substantial'. But what does that mean?

The courts have said that 'material' must mean:

- Important
- Essential or
- Relevant to the circumstances of the case

They have said that 'substantial' must mean something more than minor or trivial and, in addition, that the justification must be based on hard evidence and not on assumptions or stereotypical ideas.

Finally, it is worth pointing out that the obligation on the employer is to make reasonable adjustments. If it is not reasonable to make the adjustments – for instance, because of the cost – then the employer does not have to justify a failure to make them, although he or she would have to demonstrate why it was not reasonable to make them.

How do the Victimisation Provisions Work?

The Disability Discrimination Act contains similar, but not identical, provisions to those contained in the Sex Discrimination and Race Relations Acts to prevent women from being penalised for bringing or becoming involved with a complaint of discrimination.

The Disability Discrimination Act says that a woman will be protected under the victimisation provisions if she is treated less favourably because:

- She brought proceedings under the Act (whether to do with her employment or whether it was alleging discrimination under the provisions dealing with access to goods, facilities or services) or gave evidence or information in connection with proceedings under the Act; or
- She did anything else under the terms of the Act; or
- She alleged that someone else had contravened the terms of the Act

The woman will also be protected if the employer treats her less favourably because he or she suspects that the woman intends to do any of the above. Both disabled and non-disabled people are protected.

The Code confirms that bringing proceedings under the Act will be protected, even if those proceedings are later withdrawn. Likewise, even if an allegation that the employer has contravened the Act is withdrawn, the woman who has been victimised will still be protected. Any allegations, however, must be made in good faith.

Who Can you Sue?

Like the sex and race discrimination legislation, the Act says that the employer is liable for anything done by an employee in the course of his or her employment, whether or not it was done with the employer's knowledge and/or approval. See earlier section under direct discrimination (sex and race).

Transsexuals

Transsexuals (people who live as members of the opposite sex) are covered by the Sex Discrimination (Gender Reassignment) Regulations 1999, which are an extension of the Sex Discrimination Act to provide protection to those undergoing gender reassignment.

Under the regulations, protection is given to transsexuals against direct discrimination from the moment they indicate an intention to start the reassignment process. In addition, they have the right to compare themselves with someone absent from work due to sickness or injury if they are discriminated against during an absence when undergoing reassignment.

There are a number of exceptions which are similar to the genuine occupational qualifications of the Sex Discrimination Act (see Chapter 1 for details).

Sexual Orientation

As a result of a recent decision by the European Court of Human Rights, gays and lesbians now have some protection in the workplace.

In this case (*Smith and Grady* v. *United Kingdom*), the court said that it was unlawful to ban homosexuals from the army. It agreed with the applicants that by doing so the government had violated their right to privacy under Article 8 of the Convention on Human Rights.

Because the Human Rights Act 1998 incorporates the convention and is directly enforceable against public bodies, this decision by the European Court of Human Rights means that any policies by those bodies must not discriminate on grounds of sexual orientation. This does not include the private sector, but because tribunals and courts have to act in line with the convention, it is hard to believe that a dismissal on grounds of sexual orientation by a private employer would not be considered unfair.

In addition, there is likely to be further pressure from Europe to introduce legislation to outlaw discrimination on the ground of sexual orientation. The Amsterdam Treaty, which came into force in May 1999, says that the European Council can take action to combat discrimination based on sexual orientation (among other things).

Age Discrimination

There is no legislation in this country outlawing discrimination on the grounds of age, although the government introduced a *voluntary* Code of Practice in mid-1999, along with separate guidance for employers.

What does the Code of Practice on Age Say?

The Code urges employers to:

- Avoid using age limits or age ranges in job advertisements
- Focus on the skills of applicants rather than their age when short-listing
- Use an interviewing panel with a range of ages
- Avoid using age as a criterion in redundancy selection

In so far as tribunals may take the Code into account when deciding whether selection criteria are reasonable, it may mean that employers can no longer use length of employment as a factor, since to do so may mean that age becomes a factor, however indirectly.

Will the Code Be of Any Use to Women?

Just how much use the Code will be to women employees is open to question, given its voluntary status. But for instance, a woman made redundant on the ground of age could claim unfair selection and rely on the provisions of the Code to prove that the employer was not reasonable in using age as the sole criterion (if he or she did). It seems hard to believe that a tribunal would decide that breaching the code was within the range of reasonable responses open to an employer.

Recruitment, on the other hand, might be a more difficult argument. However, there have been cases in which employees have successfully argued that an age requirement was indirectly discriminatory.

In an important decision (*Price* v. *Civil Service Commission and anor*), the Employment Appeal Tribunal said that it was indirectly discriminatory against women to restrict recruitment to an executive officer post in the Civil Service to the ages of 17 to 28. This was because it was harder for women to gain the necessary experience by that age due to the fact that so many interrupted their careers because of childbirth.

In a more recent case (*Nash* v. *Mash/Roe Group Ltd*), a man successfully argued at an employment tribunal that the statutory upper age limit (normal retirement age or age 65) for claiming unfair dismissal was indirectly discriminatory against men. Sadly, Mr Nash died before the case was appealed and his estate is currently negotiating a settlement with the employer. Two other cases on a similar point are being appealed.

Another claim by a man seeking a statutory redundancy payment although he was over 65 has been referred by a tribunal to the European Court of Justice. If the court rules in favour of the applicant (some time in 2000), then the days of age discrimination in this country will be numbered.

Can Equal Opportunities Policies Be Enforced?

Some equal opportunities policies contain a clause barring the employer from discriminating on account of age. To succeed in a claim of age discrimination, the woman has to show that the policy is part of her contract and that the employer is in breach of it.

For instance, in a recent case (*Taylor* v. *Secretary of State for Scotland*), a prison officer claimed that forcing him to retire at 56 was contrary to his employer's equal opportunities policy. This included a clause that the employer would not discriminate on the ground of age, which both parties accepted was part of his contract. He was, however, unsuccessful in this instance because the contract gave the employer a discretion to retire people between the ages of 55 and 60, and the House of Lords said that that discretion did not contradict the intention of the equal opportunities policy not to discriminate on the basis of age.

Due to the voluntary nature of the Code, the most effective way to prevent age discrimination is through collective agreements and incorporation of the Code into contracts of employment, as in the Taylor case above.

Promotion, Transfer and Training under the SDA and RRA

It is unlawful for an employer to discriminate against a woman under the Sex Discrimination Act and the Race Relations Act in terms of promotion, transfer and training, as follows:

- In the way that the woman is given access to opportunities for promotion, transfer or training, or to any other benefits; or
- By refusing to give her access to those opportunities or deliberately omitting her from getting access to them; or
- By dismissing her or subjecting her to any other detriment

What Protection Exists?

It is important to note that protection under the legislation applies to access to opportunities for promotion, transfer, training as well as to any other benefits or facilities, plus any refusal to provide any of the above. This covers a wide range of situations. For instance, it would cover the situation where a woman was not given the chance to apply for promotion as well as those where she was not promoted because of discrimination.

What Can you Do about Discrimination in Promotion?

Rules and policies relating to promotion and appraisal can – at least in theory – be challenged on the ground of indirect discrimination (see previous section for details). The problem for women alleging indirect discrimination in promotion is that the 'requirement or condition' being imposed has to be an absolute one, according to case law. That makes it difficult to challenge a situation where the employer has said that supervisory experience is desirable, when in reality, it is essential, although it has been.

However, having said that, it is always worth trying to bring a claim, particularly in cases of sex discrimination, because the wording of the Equal Treatment Directive (which only applies to sex and not race) seems to include protection against discrimination in all aspects of promotion. That being so, women should be able to bring claims where the following criteria are used for granting access to promotion:

- Flexibility
- Mobility
- Full-time working
- Certain qualifications and experience

She would, of course, have to be able to show that the criteria favour men more than women.

What about Discrimination in Appraisals?

It stands to reason, given the above, that it is also unlawful to discriminate in appraisals of employee performance. Both the Commission for Racial Equality and the Equal Opportunities Commission recommend that any assessment criteria should be examined for any bias and the scheme monitored to assess how it works in practice. If there are obvious anomalies, the system is not working as it should.

What about Discrimination in Training Opportunities?

The same principles apply to discrimination in training. To prove that there has been discrimination, the woman just has to show that the employer failed to consider her because of her sex or her race. But if the employer can show that the decision had nothing to do with the woman's sex or race, the claim will fail.

It is also worth repeating what was mentioned in Chapter 1 – that although employers are not obliged to provide special training, both the Sex Discrimination Act and the Race Relations Act allow employers to discriminate positively in access to training. This is only allowed if at any time during the previous twelve months there was no one of that sex or race (or very few) doing that particular work.

The employer is also allowed to encourage women or members of a particular racial group to apply for certain kinds of work.

Under the Sex Discrimination Act, the employer can also provide training to people who have been out of work because of domestic or family responsibilities. This section is aimed mainly at mothers returning to work, but could equally apply to carers who have been looking after aged or sick relatives.

What if the Woman was Refused a Transfer or was Transferred against her Will?

These cases are most likely to arise in redundancy situations, when the employer has failed to consider the woman for a similar job to the one that she had been doing. In addition to a claim that the employer failed to offer suitable, alternative employment, the woman can, therefore, also bring a claim for discrimination on the ground that the employer had not afforded her access to the same opportunity for transfer as they would have to a man.

The other likely scenario for a discrimination claim is in circumstances where the woman has been transferred against her will. Depending on the circumstances, this may constitute victimisation (see above for details).

What about Discrimination in Terms of Benefits, Facilities and Services?

The Sex Discrimination Act and the Race Relations Act make it unlawful to discriminate on the grounds of sex or race in affording access to 'any other benefits, facilities or services'. The courts have said that 'benefits' mean any 'advantage' available to the employee, such as:

- Loans for house purchases
- Season tickets
- Free overalls
- Car expenses
- The right to have time off for public duties

In addition, if the employer fails to investigate or pursue adequately the woman's grievance, this can also give grounds for a claim that the employer was refused access to 'benefits, facilities or services'.

Alternatively, the woman can bring this claim on the ground that she has been 'subjected to a detriment' or for breach of an implied term of the contract (see Chapter 2 under 'Obligations on the Employer'). It is worth noting that a claim under this heading is only likely to succeed if the complaint is in relation to an *existing* benefit.

> For instance, in one case (*Clymo* v. *London Borough of Wandsworth*), the Employment Appeal Tribunal said that the woman could not complain that her employer's refusal to allow her to job share was contrary to the Sex Discrimination Act, since job sharing was not an existing facility. For some reason best known to the court, it interpreted 'opportunities and facilities' as meaning only those already in existence.

Finally, remember that sex discrimination claims about pay or other money benefits which form part of the contract have to be brought under the Equal Pay Act. There is no such distinction under the Race Relations Act which covers both types of claims.

Promotion, Transfer and Training under the DDA

The provisions under the Disability Discrimination Act are similar to the above, with one significant difference, that is, that discrimination in the form of *potential* as well as *existing* facilities and benefits is covered, thereby getting round the problem under the race and sex legislation highlighted above.

The Code which accompanies the Act provides a comprehensive list of what might constitute 'benefits':

- Canteens/meal vouchers
- Social clubs and other recreational activities
- Dedicated car parking spaces
- Discounts on products
- Bonuses/share options
- Hairdressing/clothes allowances
- Financial services
- Healthcare/medical assistance/insurance
- Transport to work/company car
- Workplace nurseries
- Rights to special leave

Family Friendly Policies

The government has recently introduced a number of so-called family friendly policies, including the EU Part-time Workers Regulations (see above) and the Parental Leave Directive.

What Parental Leave are you Entitled to?

The basic provisions for *employees* are as follows:

- Unpaid leave of at least 13 weeks available per child to each parent
- Only applicable to children born after 15 December 1999 until they reach the age of five
- In the case of multiple births, 13 weeks' leave has to be provided for each child
- In the case of adoption after 15 December 1999, the right lasts for five years or until the child reaches 18, whichever is the sooner
- In the case of a child with a disability, the right lasts until the child's eighteenth birthday (note that for the purposes of parental leave, a disabled child is one for whom disability living allowance has been awarded)
- All employees have to have been working for their employer for at least one year in order to qualify
- Employee absent on parental leave is entitled to the benefit of normal terms and conditions, except remuneration
- Employees will not lose seniority or pension rights while on parental leave
- On their return, employees must be given their old job back if the leave was for four weeks or less. If the leave was for a longer period, the employee is entitled to return to the same job or, if that is not reasonably practicable, to a similar job with the same terms and conditions and status as the old one
- Employers can ask to see evidence that the employee is the parent (or the person legally responsible for) the child, such as the birth certificate
- An employee can make a complaint to an employment tribunal if the employer unreasonably postponed her leave or prevented or attempted to prevent the employee from taking parental leave within three months of the act complained of

- Collective or workforce agreements can have effect in place of the government's model scheme, but agreements must be incorporated into contracts of employment

What does the Fallback Scheme Consist of?

The government has introduced a fallback scheme for employers and employees to follow in the event that they do not draw up their own workforce or collective agreement.

The key elements are as follows:

- Leave can be taken in blocks of one week or more, but limited to a maximum of four weeks in a year
- The exception to this is that parents of disabled children can take leave in blocks or multiples of one day
- The employee has to give notice of at least 21 days. If she wants to take more than two weeks, she has to give notice to the employer which is twice as long as the leave period
- The employer can postpone the leave if it is in the interests of the business, if a significant proportion of the workforce applies for leave at the same time, or when the employee's role is such that her absence would unduly harm the business. The employer cannot postpone the leave for longer than six months and cannot postpone the leave when an employee applies to take it immediately after the birth or adoption of the child. In that case, the employee should give 21 days' notice
- There is no statutory requirement to keep records
- If the employee changes employers, she has to re-qualify although she cannot ask for 13 weeks' leave for the same child with a different employer

Workforce or collective agreements can only improve on the model scheme – in other words, they cannot provide less favourable terms.

What about Time Off for Dependants?

As part of the government's 'family-friendly' approach, the following rights giving time off for dependants have also now been introduced for *employees*. These rights do not, however, extend to time off for dealing with domestic incidents. In other words, employees do not have the right to ask for time off to sort out a flood from a washing machine.

There is no qualifying period before the right becomes effective and there is no statutory right to payment for the time off. But equally the Act does not stipulate how much time off that an employee can take – it should just be 'reasonable'. The DTI suggests one or two days at the most.

A dependant is defined as a spouse, partner, child, parent or person in the same household as the employee (except someone who is a tenant or lodger). It also includes anyone who relies on the employee for help when ill (whether physically or mentally) or injured, or relies on the employee to make arrangements for him or her to be looked after in such circumstances.

The employee is entitled to the unpaid time off during working hours in order to 'take action which is necessary', such as:

• When a dependant falls ill, gives birth or is injured or assaulted
• To make arrangements for a dependant who is ill or injured
• When a dependant dies
• Because of the unexpected disruption or termination of arrangements for the care of a dependant
• To deal with an incident which involves a child of the employee and which occurs unexpectedly

The type of illnesses covered by the new right is not defined under the Act – the dependant just has to be ill. The illness does not have to be life-threatening, but the more serious the illness, the more likely that 'action will be necessary'.

However, the above rights will only apply if the employee tells her employer the reason for the absence as soon as practicable and how long she expects to be absent. There is no need for this to be in writing. The employee can make a claim to the employment tribunal if his employer fails to give her time off as required, as long as this is lodged within three months of the alleged failure.

4
Conduct and Rights at Work

Contract of Employment

All employees have a contract of employment (whether written or oral). They are also entitled to receive certain details about their employment in writing within two months of starting work (see Chapter 2 for details). But once provisions in a contract have been agreed, can they be changed?

Can your Employer Vary your Contract?

Under the law of contract, your employer cannot change the terms of your employment contract (whether in writing or not) without your consent. If, however, you agree to the change, it stands to reason that you cannot then sue your employer for breach of the contract.

So far, so simple. But there may be an occasion when your employer decides to go ahead and change the contract without your agreement – what do you do then? The answer is that it depends on the circumstances, as follows:

- The employer may have negotiated the change with the recognised trade union (whether you are a member or not) as part of a collective agreement. This will not always alter your contract. To find out whether it does, you need to ask either your employer or the trade union if the agreement is 'incorporated' into your contract. If it is, then your contract will be changed by the new agreement. Alternatively, look at your own contract and see if it makes reference to a collective agreement. Any change that affects your individual

contract of employment has to be brought to your notice (such as by a letter in your pay packet). Otherwise, it is ineffective
- There may be a clause in your contract that allows the employer to make changes
- You may have agreed to it by virtue of your own conduct. In other words, if you don't make any protest about the changes and keep on working, you may be deemed to have 'acquiesced' to the changes. If you disagree with them, you need to let that be known, preferably in writing to the employer – see the model letter below
- The employer might impose the change against your will. If that happens and you are unhappy with it, make that clear to the employer in writing. If you are a member of the union, contact them for advice. If not, go to your local Citizens Advice Bureau for some advice about bringing a claim for breach of contract or constructive dismissal (for more details on constructive dismissal, see Chapter 6). Trying to bring a claim for constructive dismissal is very risky and if the employer can convince a tribunal that the changes were made for good business reasons, you will lose your claim (as well as your job)
- The employer can give notice to terminate your current contract and then offer a new one containing revised terms and conditions. In those circumstances, there is no breach of contract. Your only option is to bring a claim of unfair dismissal (which is a statutory right for employees with one year's service with their employer) from the original contract

Model Letter

Dear

I have received notification from you of proposed unilateral changes to my terms and conditions of employment.

I object to any attempt to alter the terms of my contract without my consent. I do not accept the changes and although I intend to remain at work, this should not be taken as an indication of my agreement to the changes.

I believe that the variations which you are proposing constitute a breach of my contract of employment. * [I have advised my

union ... of the situation, and my regional officer ... will negotiate on my behalf].

Yours sincerely

* Delete, if not applicable

If the change fundamentally alters your contract (such as a change
from a full- to a part-time post), you can work according to the new
terms as long as you make it clear to your employer that you are
doing so under protest, on the basis that the original contract has
been terminated. You can then keep on working, but bring a claim
of unfair dismissal from the original contract.

Does your Contract Stipulate a Notice Period?

If your contract does not say anything about notice of termination,
you can rely on the following *statutory* notice periods.

Notice of termination to be given by employer:
- Continuous employment of less than four weeks – no notice
  required
- Continuous employment of more than four weeks, but less than
  two years – one week's notice
- Continuous employment of more than two years – one week's
  notice for each full year worked, up to a maximum of twelve weeks

Notice of termination to be given by employee:
- One week

But note that the notice period in your contract of employment may
be different from the above. Although it can be more generous than
the above, it cannot be any less.

Deductions from Wages

Who Can Claim?

The protection of wages provisions in the Employment Rights Act
1996 applies to workers as well as employees, meaning that anyone
who is self-employed and working under a contract is included, as

long as he or she is not a professional person (like a solicitor) or someone running their own business.

When Can an Employer Make a Deduction?

The Act allows an employer to make a deduction in the following situations:

- If it is authorised by legislation, such as deductions for tax and National Insurance, or an order made by a court directing the employer to make deductions from the worker's salary
- If the deduction is authorised by a provision in the worker's contract; but note that the worker needs to have been made aware of the term in advance. Any changes to the worker's contract to allow the employer to make a deduction must be brought to the individual attention of every worker. The term should also be very clear, otherwise the employer will not be able to make use of it: it should spell out that a deduction can be made from your wages to cover, for instance, the cost of a training course if you leave within a certain period of going on it, as opposed to just saying that you are liable for the cost of the course if you leave
- If the worker has agreed in writing to the deduction *in advance of it being made*. This is important because it stops the employer from being able to make you agree to a deduction after something has happened. For instance, if you worked in a shop and on Friday the till was £50 short, the employer cannot get you to agree on Saturday to the deduction of the shortfall from your wages

There is additional protection for individuals in retail work, making it unlawful for your employer to deduct more than 10 per cent from your gross wages, if the deduction is made because of cash shortages or stock deficiencies.

What are Wages?

It may seem obvious to you what your wages are, but for the law, things are never that straightforward. Under the legislation, there is a range of payments that can be counted as wages:

- Any fee, bonus, commission, holiday pay or other payment owing to you

- Statutory sick pay
- Statutory maternity pay
- Guarantee payments
- Payments for time off for public duties
- Medical and maternity suspension payments

Case law has stated that overtime payments, shift payments, any non-contractual bonus payments and long service awards will also qualify as wages.

Just as importantly, certain payments are specifically *excluded* from the definition of wages:

- Any loans or advance payments
- Any payments in respect of expenses
- Any payments by way of a pension, allowance or gratuity in connection with your retirement or as some other sort of compensation for the loss of office
- Redundancy payments, whether statutory or not
- Any other payment made to you, but not in your capacity as a worker
- Payments or benefits in kind, unless they have a fixed value and can be exchanged for money, goods or services, such as luncheon vouchers
- Payments in lieu of notice

What are Deductions as Far as the Law is Concerned?

In a famous case (*Delaney* v. *Staples*), the House of Lords ruled that if an employer withholds any or all of the wages which are owed to a worker, then that is an unlawful deduction. It follows, therefore, that any reduction in pay owing to a worker also constitutes a deduction.

But in *New Century Cleaning Co. Ltd* v. *Church*, the Court of Appeal said there was no deduction of wages when the company reduced the price paid to window cleaners for their regular jobs. As for commission or bonus payments, if the employee expects to receive them and they are normally paid, failure to pay is likely to be an unlawful deduction.

But if the employer makes an inadvertent error in calculating your wages, that will not constitute a deduction and you cannot therefore claim under the Employment Rights Act. That does not mean that you are not entitled to the full amount owing, just that you cannot bring a claim under the wages provision of the Employment Rights Act. In that instance, you would have to bring a breach of contract claim in the county court.

Nor are payments in lieu of notice covered by these provisions. In the above case (*Delaney* v. *Staples*), the court said that payments in lieu are not wages because they cover a period when the employment relationship has terminated. However, if your employer fails to make a payment in lieu of notice, you can bring a claim to the employment tribunal under the Employment Tribunals Extension of Jurisdiction (England and Wales) Order 1994.

Finally, if the employer claims that you owe money to him or her, can he or she deduct that sum from your wages? The answer is probably no, because there is no scope under the wages provisions of the Employment Rights Act for the employer to 'set off' any amounts which he or she claims are outstanding.

What Deductions are Excluded from the Employment Rights Act?

Certain kinds of deductions are excluded from the protection of wages provisions, as follows:

- Overpayment of wages or expenses (but see next section on recovery of overpayments)
- Statutory provisions – such as PAYE, National Insurance or deductions for attachment of earnings
- Payments to third parties on behalf of workers, such as payments to a trade union under the check off system
- Strikes and industrial action
- Money owing under a court or tribunal order by the worker to the employer

It follows, therefore, that a worker who wants to claim that any of the above deductions are unlawful can only sue for breach of contract in the county court, not in an employment tribunal.

What Happens if your Employer Overpays you?

Under the wages provisions of the Employment Rights Act, an over-payment of wages or expenses does not constitute an unlawful deduction. In other words, when your employer stops the money out of your wages, you cannot rely on the Employment Rights Act for protection. You have to pursue a breach of contract claim in the county court.

In addition, some contracts have an express term to deal with such eventualities but, even if there is none, the employer may still have a remedy. If the employer can show that the overpayment arose because of a mistake, such as an administrative or computer error (known as a mistake of fact), then he or she will be entitled to recover the money unless:

- Your employer led you to believe that the money was yours. For instance, if you tried to bring the subject to your employer's attention but were reassured that the money was yours *and*
- You spent the money in good faith, believing that it was yours to spend *and*
- The overpayment was not your fault

If the error is due to a mistake in interpreting the law, such as statutory regulations, then the employer cannot usually recover the money, unless you were well aware that you should not have received it.

National Minimum Wage Act 1998

From October 2000 all adult workers over 22 are entitled to be paid a minimum rate of £3.70 per hour before deductions, with younger workers between 18 and 21 entitled to receive a minimum of £3.20 per hour as of 1 June 2000.

Who is Covered?

Everyone over 18 is covered by the legislation which applies to workers, not just employees (see Chapter 2 for an explanation of the difference). That means that all casual workers, freelance workers, homeworkers, temporary workers, pieceworkers, sales agents and agency workers are covered by the Act, although the genuinely self-employed are excluded, as are members of the armed forces and voluntary workers.

How is it Calculated?

In order to figure out whether you have been paid the right amount, you need to work out your hourly rate of pay. You do this as follows:

$$\frac{\text{Total Pay}}{\text{Total Hours Worked}}$$

In other words, you divide the total amount you get paid by the total number of hours you have worked over a day, week or a month (known as the pay reference period), depending on whether you are paid daily, weekly or monthly.

You do not have to be paid the national minimum wage for *each* hour worked, but it must be paid on average for the time worked over any particular day, week or month.

What about Overtime Payments?

What happens if you are paid monthly and work some overtime in June and do not get paid for it until July? How do you work out your pay for June? According to the legislation, you still include the pay for the overtime in the June pay packet in your calculations, even though you did not get it until July.

How do you Work Out your Gross Salary?

The national minimum wage is based on your *gross* salary – that is, before deductions of tax and National Insurance – so you have to make sure you have the right figure before you start accusing your employer of short-changing you.

Do *not* include any of the following for calculating your gross pay. In other words, deduct all these from your hourly rate (the total sum paid to you every day, week or month divided by the number of hours you worked in that day, week or month):

- A loan
- An advance of wages
- Pension payment
- Lump sum on retirement

- Redundancy payment
- A reward under a staff suggestion scheme
- The premium element of overtime and shift pay
- Special allowances (unless consolidated into standard pay)
- Expenses
- Refund of money spent on the job
- Deduction or payment for expenditure connected with the job, such as tools, uniform, etc.
- Deduction or payment for the employer's own use or benefit
- Payments by the worker to another person connected with the job
- Accommodation above a certain limit

But *do* include the following in the calculation of your gross pay:

- Incentive pay
- Bonuses
- Tips paid through pay roll
- Income tax and NI contributions
- Deduction or payment of a penalty, for instance, because of misconduct
- Deduction or payment to repay a loan
- Deduction or payment to repay an advance of wages
- Deduction to pay for purchase of shares or securities by worker
- Deduction to recover an accidental overpayment of wages
- Deductions such as union subscription or pension contribution
- Any deduction made by employer but not for his/her use or benefit
- Payment by worker for goods and services from employer (as long as worker not required to buy them)

How Many Hours Have you Worked?

Although it may be obvious to you how many hours you have worked in a given week or month, some workers have no fixed hours which can complicate the calculations for the national minimum wage. Those workers need to know which of the hours they have worked will actually count towards the national minimum wage. They also need to know how to translate work paid by results (and not time) into an hourly figure. To figure this out, they need to know which of the following four work types they fall into.

What Type of Work do you Do – Is it Time Work?

This is work that is paid for according to periods of time – for instance, a worker who is paid according to the number of hours she is at work and which may vary from day to day. Time work rules will also apply when a person doing piece work is expected to work for a set number of hours per day. Most workers will be time workers if they are not on an annual salary.

To figure out the number of hours that will count, just add up the total number of hours you have worked in a day, week or a month. The following hours count:

- Time spent at or near the workplace, excluding rest breaks, tea and lunch breaks
- Time spent on standby or on call at or near the place of work (but not if you are at home)
- Time spent at work, even if you are unable to work because something has broken down
- Travelling time connected with the business (including rest breaks), except travel between home and work
- Training time and time spent travelling to and from it
- If you have to sleep over at work, you will be paid for any time you have to get up and work

However, periods when you are on holiday, on sick leave or on maternity leave will not count for the purposes of the minimum wage.

Take the following example:

- You have to be at work for 40 hours per week – all these hours therefore count for calculating the minimum wage
- Usually, you make garments at a rate of £1.50 per garment. As you can make three per hour, you get paid £4.50 per hour
- But sometimes you are slower and only produce two – £3.00 per hour
- As long as your weekly wage averages out at £3.70 per hour, your employer does not have to pay you more for the hours when you are only operating at £3.00 per hour, as follows:
  - 35 hours at £4.50 per hour = £157.50
  - 5 hours at £3.00 per hour =   £ 15.00
                                    £172.50
- An average of £4.31 per hour

What Type of Work do you Do – Is it Salaried Hours Work?

These are people who work basic hours under an annual contract and are paid roughly equal amounts during the year. To calculate these hours, just divide the total number of basic hours in the year by twelve (if paid monthly).

The hours that count for the minimum wage are the same as those for time workers (see above), except that absences such as rest breaks, lunch breaks, holidays, sick and maternity leave can be counted if they are included in your basic minimum hours under the contract. So, if your contract says you are employed for 35 hours per week and that includes your lunch break, then you are entitled to count that time into the number of hours you work every week or month for calculating the minimum wage.

However, if you are away on long-term sick leave and are on a *reduced* salary (or none at all), then you cannot include this time in calculating the minimum wage.

Take the following example:

- You are paid £7,200 per year as your basic salary, in regular monthly instalments of £600
- You work 40 hours per week, including rest breaks
- Your annual hours are therefore 40 x 52 = 2,080
- Every month you work 2,080 hours divided by twelve, in other words, 173 hours
- Divide your monthly salary of £600 by 173 hours to calculate whether you are being paid the national minimum wage. You are being short-changed because it works out at £3.46 per hour

What Type of Work do you Do – Is it Output Work?

These are workers who are paid by output, not by reference to time (see time workers above). Output workers include:

- Homeworkers who do piecework
- Commission workers
- Sales agents paid according to the number or value of sales they make

Employers can continue paying these workers according to the number of pieces produced, but for the purposes of the national minimum wage those figures have to be converted somehow to an hourly rate.

This is done by coming to a 'fair estimate' agreement of the number of hours you are likely to work in any day, week or month (depending on how often you are paid). The fair estimate agreement:

- Must stipulate the number of hours it is likely to take you to do the work in a given day, week or month (depending on how often you are paid)
- Must base the number of hours in the agreement on how long it takes an average worker to do the same job in order to be 'fair'. If it is clearly unfair, you can complain to a tribunal
- Should also include time spent travelling with the job. For example, the time spent travelling by a salesperson from one appointment to the next

You would therefore need to keep a record of the actual hours you have worked and make sure you agree with your employer how much you will be paid for each item produced. You can be paid according to your output, but you are entitled to be paid the minimum wage if you work the agreed 'fair estimate' hours in a given day, week or month. If you work less than those hours, you cannot expect to be paid for them. However, if you work more than the estimated hours, you will not be entitled to be paid for them either.

The benefit to employers is clear – they can limit the number of hours for which the minimum wage has to be paid. But for workers whose pay consists of commission only, a fair estimate agreement is of great benefit because even if they do not earn any commission in a given period, they will still be paid the minimum wage for the agreed estimated hours.

Take the following example:

- You are supposed to make two items an hour at £2.00 per item. The fair estimate agreement says you will work for 40 hours a week

- If you work the 40 hours, then you are entitled to be paid £148 (40 x £3.70), whatever your level of output, although if you keep to the agreement you will be entitled to £160 (40 x 2 x £2.00)
- However, if you only work 30 hours, you are only entitled to be paid for 30 hours

The only other alternative is for your employer to pay the minimum rate for each hour you have worked, regardless of how many items you produced. This will include time spent travelling on business.

What Type of Work do you Do – Is it Unmeasured Work?

This is a catch-all for any other type of work not covered by any of the above formulas and could include work where you have to do certain tasks, but where the employer does not specify any number of hours or times within which they have to be done. For instance, it may be that you only work when work is available, such as domestic staff.

To figure out the hours for which you will be paid the national minimum wage, you have to agree with your employer a 'daily average' number of working hours. The agreement has to stipulate a realistic average number of hours it is likely to take you to do the work given to you, which should include any travelling time in connection with the job (except for travel between home and work). The only other alternative is to make sure you are paid the minimum wage for each hour you have actually worked.

How do you Get Hold of Information you May Need?

Your employer has to keep records, including copies of 'fair estimate' and 'daily average' agreements, for at least three years to show that he or she is paying a rate at least equivalent to the minimum wage. You have the right to inspect, examine and copy any part of those records if you suspect you are being paid less than your legal entitlement. Simply tell your employer in writing that you want to see them and the employer must agree within 14 days. Although your employer can decide where the inspection takes place, he or she needs to let you know in good time where that will be. Unless otherwise agreed, it is likely to be at your place of work.

If your employer fails to let you see the records, you can complain to the tribunal within three months of the date of refusal. If you succeed, the tribunal can make you an award of a sum equal to 80 times the hourly amount of the minimum wage in force (£296 at present rates).

What Can you Do if your Employer Refuses to Pay you the Proper Rate?

You can complain to a tribunal that your employer has made an unauthorised deduction of wages under Part 2 of the Employment Rights Act or, alternatively, you can bring an action for breach of contract in the county court. If you bring the claim to the tribunal, you are only entitled to recover the underpayment, whereas in a county court you can also claim interest.

As long as the claim is brought within the time limit (three months), there are no limits in a tribunal on how far back the complaint can go. In a county court, claims can only go back a maximum of six years. The burden of proof is on the employer to show that he or she paid the minimum wage.

What do you Do if your Employer Takes Action against you?

You also have the right to claim automatically unfair dismissal or victimisation if your employer sacks you or takes some other action against you for trying to ensure that you receive the national minimum wage. You have the same right if your employer sacks you because you are going to become eligible to claim the national minimum wage.

Trade Union Rights

Do Trade Unions Have a Statutory Right of Recognition?

If you are a trade union member, but your employer does not talk to the trade union or bargain with it over pay or conditions in general, you now have the right to get your union recognised. You can apply for automatic recognition in cases where over half the relevant workforce are already union members, and the employer must grant it.

Where that is not the case, you need to write to the employer and make a formal request for recognition. In that case, you will have to have a ballot in which you need the support of a majority of those who vote, as well as the support of 40 per cent of the total workforce *eligible* to vote. Small employers (those with 20 or less employees) are exempt from this provision.

What about an Individual Right to Representation?

As an employee or a worker you now have the right to be accompanied in disciplinary and grievance procedures by a trade union official, whether or not your union is recognised by your employer in the workplace. If you are not a trade union member or you do not want an official to come with you, you still have the right to be accompanied by a work colleague.

Can your Employer Dismiss you for your Trade Union Activities?

It is automatically unfair:

- To dismiss you because of your membership (or non-membership) of an independent trade union
- To dismiss you for taking part (or refusing to take part) in your union's activities or proposing to do so. This protection is restricted to taking part in activities 'at an appropriate time', which means at a time agreed with the employer during working hours, or else outside working hours altogether
- To dismiss you if you can show that you were selected for redundancy because of your trade union membership or activities

What is Interim Relief?

There is a special remedy known as interim relief to protect workers dismissed for the above reasons, under which a woman can ask a tribunal at an interim hearing to re-employ her on similar terms and conditions or to keep her suspended on full pay until the full tribunal hearing. The effect of a tribunal ordering interim relief is to prevent the dismissal taking full effect before the main hearing, but the woman needs to be able to convince the tribunal that her case is likely to succeed when it comes to the main hearing. To claim interim relief, you have to lodge your claim within seven days of dismissal and have the full support of your union.

Can your Employer Take Action Short of Dismissal against you?

All employees, irrespective of their length of service, are protected against trade union victimisation in any of the following situations:

- Where the employer tries to prevent her from becoming a member or penalises her for doing so
- Where the employer tries to prevent her from being active in the union or penalises her for doing so
- Where the employer tries to make her join a trade union

Such action could include disciplining the woman, making her relocate or subjecting her to some other disadvantage. It also includes a situation where the employer gives a benefit to non-union members, but omits to provide the same benefit to union members. In other words, discrimination by omission is also included. Again, you have to show that any activities you were engaged in were at 'an appropriate time' (see above).

What Can you Do if you are Refused a Job on Union Grounds?

It is unlawful to refuse someone a job because of their *membership (or non-membership)* of a trade union. This protection applies if the employer failed to process your application or enquiry, made you withdraw, deliberately refused to offer you the job, offered the job on unreasonable terms which you rejected, or made an offer and then withdrew it. For instance, failing to respond to a telephone enquiry could be deemed a refusal of employment.

This does not, however, specifically cover the situation where an employer refuses to employ you because of your *trade union activities* in another job. But the courts have said that, although only trade union membership is covered, that must mean more than just having a membership card, otherwise the scope of the protection offered would be minimal. It can, therefore, also mean participation in the activities of the union.

Under new legislation, employers are now prohibited from drawing up lists of union activists which are circulated among employers and employment agencies preventing active trade unionists from getting work. Activists can complain to an employment tribunal if they suspect that they have been targeted and the employer will also face a criminal charge.

What Time Off are you Entitled to for Trade Union Duties and Activities?

Under the Trade Union and Labour Relations (Consolidation) Act 1992, union officials have the right to reasonable *paid* time off to carry out union duties. Union members, on the other hand, have the right to reasonable *unpaid* time off to take part in union activities. These rights only apply to employees (see Chapter 2 for an explanation) and those who work in Great Britain.

The right to time off only arises if the employee is an official or member of a recognised, independent trade union, which would not necessarily include membership of a staff association, for instance. In other words, it has to be independent of the control of an employer. The union also has to be recognised by the employer for the purposes of collective bargaining before the rights to time off apply.

What Constitutes Trade Union Duties?

The union official has the right to paid time off to carry out duties in connection with *negotiations* about any of the following for which the union is recognised:

- Terms and conditions of employment, such as pay, hours of work, holidays
- Engagement and termination of employment of workers, such as recruitment and selection, redundancy arrangements
- Allocation of work between workers, such as job grading, job evaluation and job descriptions
- Matters of discipline, such as disciplinary procedures
- A worker's membership or non-membership of a trade union, such as union involvement in the induction of new workers
- Facilities for union officials, such as arrangements for the provision of accommodation and equipment
- Machinery for negotiation or consultation, such as arrangements for collective bargaining, grievance procedures, joint consultation, etc.

The official is also entitled to time off for duties that the employer has agreed may be *carried out* by the union (such as representation at disciplinary hearings) in relation to any of the above. In other words, the employer may have refused to negotiate over disciplinary matters, but may have agreed to let officials represent their members at the hearings.

It is crucial that the duties relate to or are connected with any of the collective bargaining matters listed above for the official to be eligible to receive paid time off. Usually internal union meetings will fit the bill, but they must be authorised meetings (that is, authorised by the union) to constitute a duty. Your employer may need some evidence – such as an agenda – to persuade him or her that the meeting is relevant to some collective bargaining matter for which the union is recognised.

What about Time Off for Training for Union Officials?

To carry out their duties properly, union officials may need training and, under the law, officials have the right to paid time off for matters for which the union is recognised. However, the training must be approved by the Trade Union Congress or the official's own union. The ACAS Code of Practice on training (available from the ACAS office) gives guidance on what forms of training should be considered:

- Initial training in representational skills for newly elected officials
- Further training, particularly where the official has special respon-sibilities
- Training on changes in the structure or topics of negotiation
- Where legislative changes may affect the conduct of industrial relations

The employer has the right to see the details of a proposed course to decide whether it is relevant to the official's duties.

What Constitutes Trade Union Activities?

A member of a recognised trade union is entitled to a reasonable amount of unpaid time off to take part in activities of the union. The ACAS Code of Practice gives several examples:

- Attendance at workplace meetings to discuss and vote on the outcome of negotiations with the employer
- Meetings with full-time officials to discuss issues relevant to the workplace
- Voting in official ballots on industrial action
- Voting in union elections

When the member is acting as a representative of the union the ACAS Code suggests the following activities might be included:

- Union meetings (branch, area or regional) when some particular business of the union is being discussed
- Meetings of policy-making bodies such as the executive committee of the union
- Meetings with full-time officials to discuss issues relevant to the workplace

What Constitutes a Reasonable Amount of Time Off?

Not surprisingly, the amount of time off afforded to an official or member is not unlimited. Requests for time off need to be reasonable in all the circumstances, and unions should bear the following in mind:

- The size of the employer's organisation and the number of workers
- How the absence/s may affect production
- The impact it may have on maintaining a service, for instance, to the public
- The operational requirements of the employer
- Any safety problems it may cause

These considerations have to be weighed against the need for unions to organise effectively. Hence the importance of reaching agreements on time off where possible.

The ACAS Code of Practice stresses that unions should give as much advance notice of the training as possible to employers and supply them with as much information as possible about the course. But even if the union does so, your employer may still be reasonable in refusing the request if you ask for time off for too many officials or at a particularly busy production time.

In one case (*Hairsine* v. *Kingston upon Hull City Council*), the Employment Appeal Tribunal said that if an employee is on night duty during the course, it would be good practice to give her the whole night off in order to sleep and attend the course the following day. It would also be reasonable to allow a second night off if the course finishes in the late afternoon because it would be dangerous to allow a tired employee near machinery.

What about Payment for Time Off?

Once it is established that the time off is required to carry out trade union duties or training, the woman will be entitled to payment. If her pay does not vary with the amount of time she works, her pay slip at the end of the month will not change. But, for instance, if she is a pieceworker, she is entitled to average hourly earnings. In any event, those hourly earnings cannot drop below £3.70 per hour (see above for an explanation of the National Minimum Wage) if the woman is 21 or over.

However, problems have arisen – particularly for women – when trying to claim payment for time off which is outside working hours. The following cases illustrate the point:

In the first example (*Arbeiterwholfahrt der Stadt Berlin* v. *Botel*), Mrs Botel worked part time, but went on a union training course during work time which exceeded her normal hours. She was paid her normal part-time salary, although full-time members on the same training course were paid on a full-time basis. All were members of the staff committee and the majority of those who worked part time were women. Mrs Botel won her case because the employer could not justify the failure to compensate her for all the time spent on the course.

Mrs Lewark established a similar principle when she took her employers to the European Court of Justice (*Kuratorium für Dialyse und Nierentransplantation* v. *Lewark*). She worked part time but went on a five-day staff training course and was paid only for her part-time hours. The ECJ said that paying her for her part-time hours would deter other part-timers from attending, the majority of whom are women.

In a recent case (*Davies* v. *Neath Port Talbot County Borough Council*), the Employment Appeal Tribunal agreed that a part-time worker was entitled to receive payment for the hours actually spent on a trade union training course for health and safety representatives, not just the payment for her normal 22-hour week.

What Can you Do if your Employer Refuses to Give you the Time Off?

As a union official, you can complain to a tribunal that your employer failed to let you take reasonable time off or failed to pay you properly for the time off. As a union member, you can complain that your employer did not give you time off for union activities. These complaints have to be lodged with the tribunal three months from the date of refusal. The tribunal will only extend this time limit if you can persuade it that you made the application as soon as you could.

If the tribunal finds in your favour, they will make a declaration to that effect and if you have not been paid the full amount owing to you, then the tribunal will award whatever is owing. The tribunal also has a discretion to award you compensation, but this is usually just a token amount.

Other Public Duties

Are you Entitled to Time Off for Public and Other Duties?

As an employee, you have the right to a reasonable amount of time off during your working hours for public duties, but you do not have the right to be paid, unless your contract specifically provides for payment. The following positions come under the heading of public duties:

* Justices of the peace
* Members of a local authority
* Members of a police authority
* Members of a statutory tribunal
* Members of an NHS Trust or Health Authority
* Prison visitors
* School governors

How Much Time Off are you Entitled to?

Under the legislation you are entitled to have time off to attend meetings of the relevant body or to carry out any functions of the body. As far as magistrates are concerned, court sessions are covered, as well as any other essential duties such as visiting penal institutions or training sessions. JPs can also take on extra commitments which will be covered by the time off provisions, such as membership of a Probation Committee or a Juvenile Court panel.

What is deemed a reasonable amount of time off will depend on the duties involved in the job and the seniority of the employee within the public body. Basically, the more senior the role, the more reasonable the request for time off will be. A tribunal will also take account of the fact that some public bodies lay down minimum attendance requirements, such as court sessions for magistrates, which cannot be avoided if the individual is to carry out the essential duties of the job. You cannot necessarily expect your employer to provide all the time off for the job, so be prepared to do some of it in your own time.

What Can you Do if your Employer Refuses the Time Off?

If your employer refuses to let you have what you think is a reasonable amount of time off, you can complain to a tribunal within three months of the date of refusal. But all the tribunal can do is to make a declaration that you are entitled to the time off and award you compensation. They cannot force the employer to give you the time off, they can only make a non-binding recommendation indicating what it thinks would be a reasonable amount of time off.

How do Tribunals Decide what is Reasonable?

The dominant factor in the majority of cases which go to tribunal will be the effect that the request has on the employer's business. For instance, if you are a key worker in a small manufacturing organisation, any absences could have a serious impact on production. The greater the need for your presence at work, the more reasonable it will be for the employer to refuse the time off.

The other important factors that the tribunal will look at are the size of the employer's business and the ease with which you can be replaced. The larger the organisation, the more that will be expected of it in terms of provision of time off.

Job Mobility

As explained in Chapter 2, if you are an employee, your employer has to give you written particulars of where you are required to work. That means stipulating the place of work if there is only one or stipulating that you have to work in different sites if there are more than one. Your employer is supposed to give you this information within two months of your starting date of work.

What does your Contract Say?

If your contract specifies one particular workplace and does not include a mobility clause (that is, a clause allowing your employer to alter your workplace), then your employer cannot make you move elsewhere to work. Any attempt to do so will constitute a breach of contract. But if your contract has a mobility clause, then you will be bound by it, unless you can show that it would be indirectly discriminatory against you.

Can Job Mobility Clauses Be Discriminatory against Women?

Discrimination can occur at any stage from recruitment onwards if employers make negative assumptions about the degree of mobility of female applicants or employees, on the basis of their marital and/or family responsibilities.

In a well-known case (*Meade-Hill and National Union of Civil and Public Servants* v. *British Council*), the applicant argued that the mobility clause in her contract was indirectly discriminatory against her, since it was more difficult for women than men to move house because they are more likely to be secondary earners. Although the employer had not tried to invoke the clause, the Council had indicated that they might have to. She said she could not move because her husband, who earned a lot more than her, would not be able to earn an equivalent amount outside London. The Court of Appeal agreed that more women than men would have trouble complying with a requirement to be mobile and that the clause was therefore indirectly discriminatory in this instance (see Chapter 3 for an explanation of indirect discrimination).

Is the Mobility Clause Ambiguous?

If you cannot show indirect discrimination, then the mobility clause will be valid as long as it is written in terms which are clear and unambiguous. If you think the clause is open to dispute, then it may be worth arguing the point before a tribunal (if your employment has terminated), but you must do so within three months of the date of termination. If you are still working for the employer, you can lodge a claim with the county court within six years of the breach occurring.

But even if the clause is clear and unambiguous, your employer still has obligations towards you in the way that he or she operates the clause. For instance, he or she must give you reasonable notice that you will be expected to move job locations and must not ask you to do anything which is impossible in practice. In other words, your employer cannot expect you to move from, say, London on Friday and start work in Sheffield on Monday.

What is the Effect of a Mobility Clause in the Event of Redundancy?

Things get more complicated if you are being made redundant (see Chapter 6 for details). Essentially, redundancy takes place in three circumstances:

- Where there has been a closure of the business as a whole
- Where there has been closure of the particular workplace where the employees worked
- Where there has been a reduction in the size of the workforce for carrying out work of a particular kind

There is usually no difficulty in establishing where someone works, but it becomes more difficult when the contract contains a mobility clause.

Consider the following case (*Horst and ors* v. *High Table Ltd*) in which a number of silver service waitresses were made redundant by their employer, High Table. Although they had all been working at one location where the redundancies had taken effect, the applicants argued that there was a provision in their contracts allowing their employer to transfer them elsewhere to work which would mean they would not be redundant. However, the Court of Appeal disagreed and said although the contract contained a mobility clause, the reality was that the women had always worked in the place where the redundancies had taken place.

Can your Employer Change your Place of Work on Return from Maternity Leave?

If you decide to return to work after ordinary maternity leave, you are entitled to return to the *same* job with all the same terms and conditions. If you take additional maternity leave, you are entitled to return from leave to a job of a 'prescribed' kind.

Failure to allow an employee to return to her old job normally constitutes automatically unfair dismissal. However, the employer is allowed to offer alternative employment under a new contract, which might involve a change of workplace, in the following two circumstances:

- Where the old job is redundant, in which case the employer must offer any suitable vacancy. Failure to do so will be automatically unfair
- Where it is not reasonably practicable to offer the old job back, the employer does not have to offer a suitable vacancy, but if there is one and the employer does not offer it, the dismissal is likely to be unfair. Note that if the employer offers a suitable vacancy and the woman unreasonably refuses, there is no dismissal and she cannot bring a claim for unfair dismissal

If you accept a vacancy on different terms to the old job, you are entitled to a statutory trial period of four weeks. If at the end of that period, you decide the job is not suitable, you are still entitled to a redundancy payment (see Chapter 6 on redundancy). You also have the right to take time off for interviews.

In both cases, 'suitable' means suitable to the employee. This means that where the workplace has been changed, tribunals can take into account the domestic problems of having a young baby, the increase in childcare costs and the increase in travelling time to get to a new workplace. So if your employer refuses to give you your job back and neither of the two exceptions apply, you should put in a claim for automatically unfair dismissal and sex discrimination.

Office Romances

Can your Employer Interfere?

You may think that having a relationship at work has nothing to do with your employer, but when it starts to affect his or her business, the employer will have a legitimate right to get involved. If the relationship breaks down, there may be friction between the two parties in the workplace or particular problems may arise when their personal lives start to spill over into work.

> For instance, in a case involving two police officers (*Finn* v. *South Wales Constabulary*), the woman brought a claim of sex discrimination against her employer on the basis that her employer's investigations into the relationship had invaded her privacy. The tribunal said, however, that her employers were entitled to investigate allegations from other officers that the relationship was causing tension and was impairing operational efficiency.

The Human Rights Act 1998 may strengthen the arguments put forward by employees that investigations by employers are an invasion of privacy.

Is it Fair to Dismiss Employees Having a Relationship?

In circumstances where employees are under a professional duty not to enter personal relationships with, say, patients or students, employers are entitled to investigate any breach of that duty. If the employer subsequently dismisses the employee, a tribunal is likely to find the dismissal fair as long as the employer carried out a reasonable investigation and followed an adequate procedure.

If the employer only dismisses one of the employees having the relationship, this may well lead to a claim of sex discrimination, simply because the man and the woman will have been treated differently (unless, of course, the relationship is between two employees of the same sex in which case neither will be able to argue sex discrimination). It is worth noting that, if the employer adopts a policy of always dismissing the less senior of the two employees, this may lead to a claim of indirect discrimination as the woman is more likely to be the junior colleague.

Not surprisingly, if your employer finds you having sex at work – or some other form of intimate physical contact – such behaviour is likely to lead to dismissal on the basis of gross misconduct, whether or not the behaviour took place within office hours. A tribunal is likely to find that this was a reasonable response on the part of the employer.

What about Husband and Wife Teams?

In some industries it is common for husband and wife teams to be employed. Their contracts usually state that if one partner is dismissed, then it is fair to dismiss the other. The courts have clarified that the converse is also the case – that if one is re-instated, then so should the other. This situation is, however, different from that of a husband and wife who just happen to work together.

Can your Employer Forbid you from Having a Relationship at Work?

In the United States, some companies have drawn up contracts which either forbid or try to regulate office relationships. Although these have not taken hold in the UK, some firms operate a policy whereby, for instance, a manager is required to own up to a relationship with someone in a more junior position.

In theory, this is to give the employer a chance to monitor the situation and ensure that the relationship does not get out of control. However, whether there is a contract or a policy in existence, the employer is still dependent on the employee owning up to the relationship which, in the circumstances, seems unlikely.

Clothing and Appearance

It is quite possible that your employer tells you to dress in a certain way at work, either because you have contact with the public or because of health and safety reasons. If you are dismissed for refusing to comply with that code, you may be able to bring a claim of unfair dismissal (see Chapter 7) or an allegation of sex or race discrimination, depending on the circumstances.

What Can you Do if your Employer Dismisses you?

If your employer dismisses you because of your image at work, you may want to bring a claim of unfair dismissal, although to do so you have to have been employed for a year or more.

It is worth knowing that your employer needs to be able to produce a convincing reason for imposing some sort of dress or image code. For instance, an electrician who was dismissed for refusing to have his hair cut was held to have been unfairly dismissed because the tribunal said his appearance was not detrimental to the employer's business nor to the way he did his work.

Poor personal hygiene can also lead to dismissal. In a recent case, a reporter was sacked by his employer, having been warned on three occasions about his offensive BO and scruffy appearance. The employer won the case on the basis that the reporter came into contact with the public and acted as an ambassador for the company.

What about Health and Safety Regulations?

If your employer has imposed rules because of health and safety requirements which you fail to observe, then your dismissal is likely to be fair. However, employers have a duty to look into any complaints you may have about safety equipment and try to remedy them before disciplining you. For instance, a woman who could not wear safety goggles with her glasses was found to have been unfairly dismissed because her employers did not investigate her complaints.

Can you Bring a Claim of Sex/Race Discrimination?

It will be more difficult to win your case if your contract states that you have to wear a uniform (for whatever reason) and you refuse. However, you may be able to bring a claim of sex discrimination if, for instance, you believe the uniform you have to wear is demeaning or offensive to you and a man would not be required to dress in the same way. Alternatively, you may be able to bring a claim of race discrimination, if, for instance, the employer insists that you wear a skirt when your religion forbids you to show your legs.

What do you Have to Prove in a Complaint of Sex Discrimination?

If your employer tries to apply different rules to men as opposed to women, then you may be able to bring a claim of sex discrimination (see Chapter 3 for an explanation of direct and indirect discrimination). But in order to succeed you have to be able to show that you have been treated differently to a man and suffered a detriment.

In one case (*Schmidt* v. *Austicks Bookshops Ltd*), there was a rule that female members of staff who came into contact with the public were not allowed to wear trousers. Miss Schmidt was dismissed for refusing to comply with the rule. The Employment Appeal Tribunal said that she had not been discriminated against because there were also restrictions on the appearance of male staff.

Since that case, tribunals have often found that employers can impose different dress codes for men and women as long as there is a set of rules that apply to each. The result has been that employers can exercise a lot of discretion in controlling the image of their establishment, usually based on a very conventional view of what men and women should look like.

So men with long hair and earrings are out (*Smith* v. *Safeway plc*), as are women wearing badges proclaiming their lesbian identity which might cause offence to fellow employees and customers (*Boychuk* v. *HJ Symons Holdings Ltd*).

In one case involving a male transvestite, the Employment Appeal Tribunal said that he was not discriminated against when his employers refused to let him wear women's clothes at work because women were not allowed to attend work dressed as men.

Recently, however, a woman employed at a golf club brought a case of discrimination after her employer told her to go home and change out of a trouser suit. The tribunal found in her favour.

The upshot of all this is that, generally, as long as restrictions on dress and appearance are applied equally to men and women, an employer will not be in breach of the Sex Discrimination Act even if the restrictions are different. It is only where a dress code is imposed

on one sex, but not the other, that the employer is open to a claim
of direct discrimination.

What about a Claim of Race Discrimination?

The courts have said that an employer cannot require employees to
comply with a dress code which contradicts their religious or cultural
beliefs, except where health and safety considerations apply. This is
the case whether the discrimination is direct or indirect (see Chapter
3 for an explanation). However, employees have to constitute a racial
group under the Race Relations Act in order to be protected by it.
Rastafarians, for instance, are not. As a result, a black Rastafarian had
no protection under the Act when his employer dismissed him for
wearing a hat at work which he wore because of his religious beliefs.

If an employer imposes a dress code, such as a requirement that
everyone should wear a uniform, then he or she has to be able to
justify it if it causes problems for some employees. For instance, a
requirement that all female staff wear a uniform which consists of an
overall over a skirt would be likely to cause problems for Muslim
women whose religion dictates that they wear trousers. In these circumstances, it would be difficult for an employer to provide a
justification.

However, when it comes to health and safety requirements,
employers can usually provide a reasonable justification for
imposing certain dress requirements, such as hard hats on a
building site or at a factory. In one case involving British Steel
(*Dhanjal* v. *British Steel General Steels*), a Sikh was dismissed for
refusing to wear a hard hat at the steel factory where he worked.
The tribunal said that health and safety considerations had to
prevail over the Race Relations Act.

Searches, Surveillance and Drug Testing

Can your Employer Search you?

For once, the law is quite clear. Your employer has no right to subject
you to a physical search, whatever the circumstances, without your
consent. If you are searched against your will, even if you do not
suffer any personal injury, the employer is guilty of assault and you
can sue for damages.

Can you Refuse to Be Searched?

In reality, however, if you refuse to be searched and your employer cannot force you, then his or her suspicions are likely to be increased and he or she is likely to do one of two things:

* Use your refusal as evidence against you in a disciplinary hearing
* Call the police, if the matter is sufficiently serious, to resolve it

If you exercise the right to refuse to be searched and your employer uses your refusal to instigate disciplinary proceedings, you may want to resign and claim constructive dismissal (see Chapter 6 for an explanation). But be aware that this can be a very risky approach as you may not succeed in your claim and you will, by then, have lost your job.

What if your Employer Has the Right to Search you?

Even if your employer has the contractual right (see under Human Rights below) to subject you to a physical search, then it must be carried out in a reasonable way. For instance, it should be done in privacy and by another woman. There should also be limits to which the employer can go – even if there is a contractual right to search, this does not mean that he or she can carry out an intimate strip search. In those extreme circumstances, you may want to resign and claim both constructive dismissal and sex discrimination on the basis that a man would not have been treated in the same way.

Is the Human Rights Act 1998 Any Help?

From October 2000, public sector employees may be able to make a claim under the Human Rights Act 1998 which guarantees, among other things, the right to privacy. Some civil liberties lawyers take the view that a contractual clause allowing an employer to search employees violates that right.

Can your Employer Spy on you?

There is no specific law to prevent employers from spying on their workforce. That means that employers can introduce electronic cameras and other monitoring, for whatever reason, without your consent, or in some cases, even without your knowledge.

However, in extreme circumstances you may be able to claim that the surveillance constitutes a form of harassment. In a recent case (*Garbett & ors v. Sierotko*), three women successfully brought claims of sexual harassment against their employer who had secretly videoed them in the shop's toilet for his own sexual gratification.

You may also be able to claim – depending on the circumstances – that the surveillance constitutes a breach of the implied term of trust and confidence by the employer. However, to do so you would have to resign and claim constructive dismissal. If you lose your claim, you would, in that situation, also have lost your job.

To try to curb the worst excesses of surveillance, your best bet is to join a union in the hope that it can persuade the employer to sign up to a collective agreement which sets out a basic code to be followed.

What about Telephone Monitoring?

If you discover that your calls are being monitored without your consent, you have very little redress. You may, however, be able to rely on the Human Rights Act 1998 once it is introduced in October 2000, but note that it only imposes a duty on public authorities, not private employers, to act in accordance with the European Convention on Human Rights. For employees, the main significance of the convention is that it provides a right of privacy.

Take the case of Alison Halford (*Halford v. United Kingdom*), a senior police officer, who persuaded the European Court of Human Rights that intercepting telephone calls from her office was a violation of her right to privacy contrary to Article 8(1). Ms Halford had to take her claim all the way to Europe because the Human Rights Act was not available to her at that time.

A word of caution, however. Although Alison Halford was successful, other workers – such as those working in call centres – may not be. This is because the extreme form of telephone monitoring to which they are subject may be too far removed from the definition of a private interest to be able to rely on the right to privacy.

In addition, Ms Halford had not been warned that calls made using the internal telephone system were liable to be intercepted. In call centres, if employees are warned that their calls may be monitored (usually for quality control purposes), then their right to privacy no longer exists. It is an irony that the more that workers are subject to constant intrusive surveillance, the harder it is to argue that they have a reasonable expectation of privacy.

However, all courts and tribunals will be required to interpret the law to comply with the Act, and this may have implications for an employee who discovers that his or her telephone conversations have been monitored. If you resign and claim constructive dismissal (not a course of action to be recommended unless you have another job to go to), you may be able to rely on the right to privacy by arguing that your employer's conduct amounted to a breach of trust and confidence.

Would a Collective Agreement Help?

If you are in a union, you may find it helpful to draw up a collective agreement with your employer to deal with telephone calls. The policy should address the following points:

- The type of calls that you can make at work – such as quick calls to sort out domestic arrangements
- The timing of the calls you can make – for instance, your employer may only agree to let you make calls during your breaks
- Where the calls can be made from – in other words, whether they can be made from the phone on your desk (if you have one) or whether you have to use a public phone. In the case of the latter, the employer would have to ensure that a sufficient number of these were installed
- Any disciplinary measures that the employer can take in the event of a breach of the policy

Can your Employer Subject you to a Drug Test?

As with searches, employers have no right to compel their employees to take a drug test unless there is a clause in the contract allowing them to do so. If the employer forces an employee to undergo a test in the absence of an express provision, that would constitute a criminal offence. You could also sue in the civil courts for damages.

Is there Specific Health and Safety Legislation?

There are specific pieces of legislation which allow for drug testing in certain circumstances, covering workers who drive or operate machinery. For instance, under the Transport and Works Act 1992, it is a criminal offence for workers such as drivers and signallers to be under the influence of alcohol or drugs at work. The police can carry out tests if there is a suspicion that the operator is 'unfit to work'. There is also a requirement under the 1994 Safety Critical Work Regulations for employers to ensure that railway staff are physically fit.

What if your Contract Allows the Employer to Test you?

If your employment contract expressly permits drug or alcohol testing and you refuse a request to undergo a test, any subsequent dismissal is likely to be fair because your failure to agree would amount to a refusal to obey a lawful order. Basically, provided that your employer can show that drugs or alcohol are likely to affect your performance or your employer's reputation adversely and he or she carries out a reasonable investigation, the dismissal is likely to be fair. Dismissal may be either on the basis of misconduct or competence.

Sickness at Work

Just because you are sick does not mean that your employer has the right to dismiss you. Equally, however, if your absence becomes damaging to your employer's business, a court may decide that your employer was reasonable to dismiss you, after going through all the appropriate procedures. Not surprisingly, there is a difference in the way that your employer is required to deal with short-term, intermittent absences as opposed to a long-term absence.

How Should your Employer Deal with Short-term Absences?

If you are taking off a series of individual days from work, your employer is likely to start investigating your sickness pattern. Some employers have a system whereby an investigation is automatically triggered after a certain number of days have been taken off. However, it would not be fair to dismiss you after such an investigation without giving you the chance to give your side of the story or without giving you the chance to improve. Your employer should also give you a time scale in which to improve and explain the consequences if you do not.

Should your Employer Issue you with a Warning?

Although warnings may seem inappropriate in cases of absence due to illness, the employer may well be justified in doing so, particularly if your absences are for no more than a day or two at a time and hence do not require medical certificates.

However, the warnings should be sympathetically worded if it is clear that you are suffering from an underlying medical problem and your employer should make clear what will happen if the absences continue. For instance, if you suffer from dysmenorrhoea (painful periods), you may find that you are taking one or two days off at a time from work on a regular basis. Your employer needs to understand that you are suffering from a genuine medical condition and are not malingering.

Do you Have the Right to Appeal against a Dismissal?

Even if you have a very poor attendance record, you should be given the chance to appeal against the decision to dismiss. If your employer fails to let you appeal and you bring a claim of unfair dismissal (assuming you have one year's continuous employment), the tribunal will take that into account when considering whether the dismissal was fair. If you have a contractual right of appeal, then your argument is even more likely to succeed.

Is your Employer Obliged to Obtain Medical Evidence for Short-term Absences?

In general, there is no obligation on the part of your employer to obtain medical evidence in cases of intermittent illness. But if in the course of an investigation an underlying medical condition becomes evident then your employer should seek a proper medical opinion.

If it turns out that there is unlikely to be an improvement in your condition, then the employer should treat it as a long-term illness (see below). If the condition is not long term but is genuine, such as in the case of dysmenorrhoea, then your employer should treat you sympathetically. If you are dismissed, you should bring a claim for unfair dismissal and sex discrimination.

How Should your Employer Deal with Long-term Absences?

If you suffering from a long-term illness, the Disability Discrimination Act 1995 may provide some protection, that is, if you are suffering from a physical or mental impairment that has a substantial and long-term adverse effect on your ability to carry out your normal day-to-day activities (see Chapter 3 for details).

Otherwise, if you are dismissed because of a long-term illness, the dismissal may well be fair under section 98(2)(a) of the Employment Rights Act 1996. For the dismissal to be fair, your employer should:

• Discover the true medical condition
• Consider alternative employment
• Consult with you

How Can your Employer Find Out about your Medical Condition?

First of all, your employer must ask for your consent to consult either your GP or the company doctor about your medical condition. Your records are confidential and a doctor cannot disclose them without your consent.

The Access to Medical Reports Act 1988 gives further protection if your employer asks for a medical report for employment or insurance purposes. Under the Act:

• You have the right to be told that your employer has requested a report
• You have to give your consent in writing
• You have the right to see the report, although you may have to pay a small fee
• You are allowed to correct any errors in the report and can even withhold your consent to it being forwarded to your employer

However, if the employer decides to get a report from a doctor who has never looked after you, then the provisions of the Act do not apply. This is because the Act only applies to doctors who are or have been responsible for your clinical care.

What if the GP and Company Doctor Disagree?

In cases where the reports of the company doctor and that of your GP conflict, tribunals have said that it is reasonable for your employer to take the advice of the company doctor who knows you and the workplace. But if the company doctor recommends that your employer gets a report from an independent consultant and he or she fails to do so, then any dismissal is likely to be unfair.

Can you Refuse to Comply with a Request for a Report?

If you refuse to comply with a request for a report from your doctor (or any other doctor, for that matter), there is little more that your employer can do to investigate your long-term illness. It may then be fair to dismiss you either for 'capability' (that is, you are no longer capable of doing the job) on the basis of whatever limited medical evidence is available, or 'conduct' for refusing to obey a lawful or reasonable instruction.

Does your Employer Have to Find Suitable Alternative Employment for you?

If you cannot go back to your old job after a period of sickness or are unable to carry on with the same job because of a medical condition, your employer must at least *try* to find some alternative employment for you. That obligation is even greater if it turns out that you are protected by the Disability Discrimination Act 1995. However, there are limits to the obligations on employers to find other work for you and, needless to say, they do not have to create a vacancy for you.

Nor do employers necessarily have to follow the advice contained in the medical report about your future employment as the courts have said that medical evidence is just one factor among many which management have to consider. The ultimate decision whether to dismiss is a management one, not a medical one.

Does your Employer Have to Consult with you before Dismissal?

If you are off on long-term sick leave, warnings about your state of health are clearly inappropriate. Instead, your employer should consult with you regularly throughout the period of sickness absence.

In one well-known case (*East Lindsay District Council* v. *Daubney*), the Employment Appeal Tribunal said that unless there were very exceptional circumstances you should be consulted and given an opportunity to state your case, otherwise the dismissal is likely to be unfair.

The House of Lords confirmed the importance of consultation in the case of *Polkey* v. *AE Dayton Services Limited*. Basically, it is for the tribunal to decide what is necessary in the circumstances, but if it is inadequate then the dismissal will be unfair.

Can you Be Dismissed while in Receipt of Contractual Sick Pay?

It is a commonly held misapprehension that your employer cannot dismiss you while you remain entitled to contractual sick pay. If you are lucky enough to benefit from such a scheme and your employer dismisses you before it comes to an end, it will just be one factor in evaluating the overall fairness of the dismissal.

There have, however, been a number of cases recently which have made it more difficult for employers to dismiss employees on contractual sick leave.

For instance, in a recent Scottish case (*Hill* v. *General Accident Fire and Life Assurance Corporation plc*), the court said that the employer has to have a proper reason for dismissing you, not just a desire to stop paying you sick pay. In this particular case, the court said that the employer was not in breach of contract for dismissing an employee for redundancy while he was on sick leave and in receipt of sick pay. But equally it made clear that an employer could dismiss an employee on sick leave who was still entitled to receive contractual sick pay.

In a case to do with pregnancy (*Halfpenny* v. *IGE Medical Systems*), the Court of Appeal said that since Mrs Halfpenny had not exhausted her contractual entitlement to sick leave her employers had no lawful reason to dismiss her. This is a surprising (although welcome) conclusion, but is only likely to be of use to employees with cases which have something to do with pregnancy.

What if you are Dismissed for a Pregnancy-related Illness?

If you have to take time off work because you have a pregnancy-related illness and your employer dismisses you, you should bring a claim of automatically unfair dismissal and sex discrimination.

Recently, a woman was dismissed after taking time off because of an ectopic pregnancy. The tribunal said that sex discrimination and unfair dismissal rights apply equally to women who are absent in these circumstances as they do in any other pregnancy-related situations.

Are you Entitled to Receive Notice while on Sick Leave?

Remember that if you are dismissed on ill-health grounds, you are still entitled to receive pay in lieu of notice.

Data Protection Act 1998

What does the Act Do?

The Data Protection Act 1998 presents workers and their unions with the opportunity of discovering information held about them by their employers. Unlike the old 1984 Act, which this statute repeals, the new Act:

- Is not restricted to information held on computer
- Is extended to any information relating to an individual which is 'readily accessible'

This seems to mean:

- Any paper or computerised records (including microfiches) which are accessible
- Film and tape recordings

During debates in parliament, the government suggested that papers or files which were not organised in any particular way and were not 'readily accessible' would not come within the remit of the Act. However, this seems a dubious line of argument.

Who or what is the Act Supposed to Protect?

The major purpose of the Act is to regulate when and how information relating to individuals may be obtained, held, used and disclosed; in other words, how it may be processed. Central to the Act is the concept of 'personal data' which means information from which a living person can be identified. This statutory definition applies to a very wide range of personal information held by employers on their employees, including expressions of opinion, and would therefore cover any adverse comments placed on the employee's personnel file.

How Can you Be Sure that Sensitive Data about you is Protected?

The Act introduces special rules on the processing of so-called 'sensitive data'. This includes information about a person's:

- Racial or ethnic origins
- Political opinions
- Religious or other beliefs
- Trade union membership
- Health or sexual life

Processing of such data will only be permissible in a number of defined situations, which include the following:

- If the data subject (the person to whom the information pertains) gives her explicit consent
- If required by law
- In connection with legal proceedings
- For the administration of justice
- For the purpose of equal opportunities or ethnic monitoring
- For medical purposes
- To protect the vital interests of the data subject or someone else, but the data controller (the person who holds and processes the information) cannot get the data subject's consent for certain, specified reasons
- If the data subject has deliberately made the information public

Personal sensitive information cannot be used, therefore, to draw up blacklists of trade union activists or to keep information about an employee's political or religious beliefs. If you believe your employer is holding and using sensitive information about you, you have the right to challenge him or her in court. However, you are likely to need the help of your trade union or a lawyer for this.

What Principles do Employers Have to Comply with when Processing Data?

When processing personal data, the data controller has to comply with a set of data protection principles, as follows:

- Data must be processed fairly and lawfully. For instance, it cannot be used if it was obtained by deceiving or misleading someone
- It should only be obtained for specified, lawful purposes
- It should be relevant and not excessive in relation to the purpose for which it is kept
- It should be accurate and up to date
- It must not be kept longer than is necessary
- It should be processed in accordance with the data subject's rights under the Act
- It should be protected against unauthorised or unlawful processing
- It must not be transferred to a country outside the EU

Given the above principles, there is probably plenty of scope for challenging the way in which your employer processes personal data, not least on the basis of keeping material on file which is out of date or keeping data which is no longer relevant. Remember that your personal data should not be processed without your consent, unless it is necessary to meet a legal obligation on the part of the employer or for some legitimate interest pursued by the data controller.

What Rights do you Have to Access Information about you?

Under the Act, you have certain rights, if you make a written request and pay a small fee:

- To be told whether any information about you is being processed by or on behalf of the data controller

- If so, to be told what data is being processed, why and to whom it may be disclosed
- To be given a copy of the data
- To be given any information as to where the data came from
- To be told of the logic behind any decision which has been taken in complete reliance of automatic means (see below)

Despite the above rights it is worth noting that confidential references *given* by an employer are exempt, although confidential references supplied to and *held* by an employer are not.

What if your Employer Makes Decisions Based Solely on Automatic Processing?

If your employer processes personal data about you using automatic means only (such as evaluating performance at work), you are entitled to find out why. This is to enable you to find out whether personal information has been properly processed and allows you to stop an employer from taking decisions based solely on automatic processing.

If you want to stop the employer from making decisions using automatic processing, you can serve him or her with a prohibition notice stating that you do not want to be subject to purely automated decision-making procedures, if those procedures might have a significant impact on you. But even if you do not serve a notice, you still have the right to be informed that a decision using purely automated processing has been made about you. You then have the right, within 21 days from that date, to require the data controller to reconsider the decision or take a new one using a non-automated process. The data controller then has to respond to you within 21 days specifying what steps they are going to take in response.

Can you Stop your Employer Processing Data about you?

You have the right to require your employer to stop processing personal data about you on one of the following grounds:

- The processing is causing (or is likely to cause) substantial damage to you or someone else
- The damage is unwarranted

You must give written notice of your request and within 21 days of receiving it the data controller has to give a written response stating that he or she has complied, or if not, why not. The above right does not apply where you had already given your consent to the data being processed, where it is necessary for the performance of a contract to which you are a party or to comply with some legal obligation on the part of the data controller.

If you suffer damage as a result of any breach of the Act, you are entitled to compensation which will most likely be limited to financial loss and possibly injury to feelings or distress.

Can you Use the Act to See a Reference?

Confidential references are exempt from the rights of access to information set out above. In other words, you cannot use the Data Protection Act to force your employer to show you a reference he or she has written on your behalf, even if you suspect that the contents are inaccurate.

However, you can ask the employer to whom the reference was supplied to disclose it to you, as long as, by doing so, he or she does not disclose the source of the reference. So if you want to see a reference you have to go to the person to whom it has been supplied, although he or she does not have to let you see it without the referee's consent.

What Action Can you Take if Data Being Held on you is Inaccurate?

You can apply for a court order requiring a data controller to rectify, erase or destroy any personal data about you which is inaccurate. Where practicable, the court can also order the data controller to notify anyone to whom the data was disclosed to let them know that it was inaccurate.

If you suffer damage because of a data controller's breach of the Act, you will be entitled to compensation.

Human Rights Act 1998

The Act, which incorporates the Convention on Human Rights into domestic law, guarantees a range of individual rights and freedoms to people. These include the right to life, the right to privacy, freedom of religion, expression, association and assembly. In addition, the state is not allowed to subject its citizens to torture, inhuman or degrading treatment, nor to deprive them of access to justice or a fair trial.

Although this legislation may not seem to have much relevance to employment law, it is probably worth using it in a number of different circumstances; for instance, intrusive surveillance may be a violation of your right to privacy, and harassment at work may be a violation of your right not to be subjected to inhuman or degrading treatment.

Although you can only bring a direct challenge against a public sector authority, this does not mean that the courts can ignore the Act when deciding claims between two private parties. This is because courts are included in the definition of public authorities and have to act in a way that is compatible with the Act. They will, therefore, be under pressure to interpret the law in accordance with the Act at all times.

5
Health and Safety at Work

Health and safety is dominated by men. Official statistics on reportable accidents highlight the health and safety dangers facing male workers in traditional industries, but very little is known about stress, repetitive strain injury and violent assaults, all of which are more likely to affect women. Equally, safety standards are based on the needs of men, as is the equipment produced for the protection of workers. Consider the case of the policewoman who had a breast reduction because of the pain caused by the safety equipment she was supposed to wear during dangerous operations.

Developments at European level have finally resulted in the introduction of a number of regulations which may be of use to women in the workplace. However, many of them are not that well known and have subsequently not been used to the advantage of women. If you find that your employer is in breach of any of the following legislation, contact your trade union or a lawyer straight away.

The Common Law

First of all, there is the common law – that is, law made by judges and not governed by Acts of Parliament. The most important common law duty with regard to health and safety is the duty of care which the employer owes to the employee.

What is your Employer's Duty to you under the Common Law?

Basically, employers have a duty to take reasonable care to protect their employees from the risk of a foreseeable injury, disease or death at work. If an employer knows of a health and safety risk, or should have known, he or she will be liable if an employee is killed, injured or suffers illness as a result of the risk for which that employer failed to take reasonable care.

Can you Sue your Employer under the Common Law?

In the event of an accident, injury or disease you can sue your employer for negligence if you suffered harm and it was foreseeable that you would. However, to pursue such a claim you will need to ask either your trade union or a personal injury lawyer for advice.

Domestic Legislation

What are the Obligations on Employers under the Health and Safety At Work Act 1974?

Under the 1974 Act, employers have a duty 'to ensure, *so far as is reasonably practicable*, the health, safety and welfare at work of all his employees'. They must therefore ensure:

* That they employ competent staff
* That they provide a safe system of work as well as safe premises, plant and equipment

While this section appears rather imprecise, an employer's duties are in reality complex and far-reaching and can be used in a wide variety of circumstances to ensure employees' safety (see under the section on violence below).

In particular, employers must:

* Provide health and safety information, instruction, training and supervision to employees
* Consult safety representatives of recognised trade unions about health and safety arrangements
* Ensure that their activities, their premises, plant and machinery do not endanger anybody

- Not charge employees for anything done, or for equipment provided, for health and safety purposes

In determining what is or is not 'reasonably practicable', the courts try to assess whether the expense involved in minimising or eradicating the risk is disproportionate to the actual risk. The burden lies with the employer to show that it was not reasonably practicable to avoid the risk of injury.

What are the Obligations on Employees under the Health and Safety At Work Act?

Employees also have obligations under the legislation to take reasonable care for the health and safety, not only of themselves, but also of other people who may be affected by their acts or omissions at work. But it is worth noting that employees' conduct will be judged by the courts in relation to the training given by their employers, the resources available and the level of authority which they enjoy.

European Legislation

The Management of Health and Safety At Work Regulations 1992

Has your employer done a risk assessment?

These regulations, effective from 1 January 1993, require all employers and self-employed people to carry out a risk assessment of their workers and others affected by what they do. This will involve:

- Identifying the hazards present (such as work related upper limb disorders or RSI), and
- Evaluating the extent of the risks involved

The assessment should ensure that all risks in the workplace are addressed and should cover all groups of employees, plus others such as office staff, night cleaners, maintenance staff, security guards and visitors. It should also identify groups of workers who might be particularly at risk, such as young or inexperienced workers, as well as taking account of existing preventive measures.

Has your employer made a record of the findings of the risk assessment?
Once an assessment has been carried out under these regulations, employers with five or more employees are required to record any significant findings which should include:

- A list of major hazards
- The existing control measures in place
- The extent to which they control the risks
- Any groups of employees at risk

The employer is then required to monitor and review the measures put in place. The level of detail in the assessment should be broadly proportionate to the risk. The purpose is not to catalogue every trivial hazard, but to encourage employers to know the hazards in their workplace.

Has your employer done a survey of employees' health?
Under the same regulations, employers also have to survey their employees' health, particularly in the following circumstances:

- Where there is an identifiable disease or adverse health condition related to the work concerned
- Where valid techniques are available to detect indications of the disease or condition
- Where there is a reasonable likelihood that the disease or condition may occur
- Where surveillance is likely to improve the protection of the health of the employees to be covered

Every employer must also establish procedures to be followed in the event of serious or imminent danger and provide his or her employees with information on the risks identified by the assessment and the preventive measures taken.

What obligations do employees have?
Employees also have duties under the regulations, namely to use any machinery or equipment in accordance with any training received. They must also inform the employer and other employees of a work situation which poses a risk to health and safety.

What about pregnant workers?

Under new amended regulations in 1994 – the Management of Health and Safety At Work (Amendment) Regulations – the assessment must look at risks to women in the workforce who are of child-bearing age, whether pregnant or not. See Chapter 3 for more details.

Are these regulations of any use in real life?

The answer is a resounding yes. These regulations are very versatile and can be used to address just about any problem in the workplace because of the onus on the employer to carry out a risk assessment.

For instance, your employer has to do an assessment of risks involved in any work which could lead to work-related upper limb disorders and then take action to eliminate or reduce, as far as possible, the likelihood of that occurring. If he or she does not do so, and someone suffers an injury or illness as a result, then the employer is very likely to be liable.

But more importantly, the regulations can be used to prevent injuries and illnesses from occurring in the first place by making sure that you force your employer to carry out the assessment before anyone suffers harm. If he or she refuses to do so, you can report them to the Health and Safety Executive (for details, see Useful Addresses at the end of the book).

The Manual Handling Operations Regulations 1992

What do these regulations say about lifting and carrying at work?

These regulations, which came into force on 1 January 1993, provide that an employer shall, so far as is reasonably practicable, avoid the need for employees to undertake any manual handling operations which could present a risk of injury.

Manual handling means: any transporting or supporting of a load by hand or by bodily force, such as lifting, putting down, pushing, pulling, carrying or moving.

The employer must take account of:

- Posture
- Twisting movements
- Stooping

- Excessive lifting
- Lowering
- Pushing and pulling
- The different lifting capacities of men and women

Where it is impossible to avoid such an operation, the employer has to make an assessment of the risk and then take steps to reduce the risk of injury. For instance, if you are a nurse or a care assistant, your employer has an obligation to carry out an assessment of the premises where you are working, the needs of the client and the capability of staff assigned to that client.

As women have different capabilities to men, they should not be asked to lift the same weights as their male counterparts. As a general rule of thumb, women should only lift about two-thirds of the weight that men lift.

Hoists should be provided where possible and staffing levels reviewed as part of the assessment. The assessment should be regularly reviewed as the needs of the client change over time.

Do employers have to comply with the manual handling regulations?

If the employer fails to do any or all of what is required under the regulations, he or she is likely to be found liable in the event of injury to an employee if the harm done is as a result of that failure. For instance, a clerical worker at a London police station was recently awarded £400,000 in compensation for injuries to her back which she sustained lifting boxes of stationery. She had received no training other than watching a video on the subject.

In addition, the employer could face further liability in a situation where one of two employees, as a result of a defective lifting technique by one of them, injures the other while lifting together. The employer would be vicariously liable for the negligence of one, and possibly liable for the injury of the other, if it can be shown that the negligent employee had not received adequate or appropriate training.

Does your employer have a duty to warn you of the risks involved in lifting?

The duty on the employer to warn his or her employees of risk is far-reaching.

In one case (*Colclough* v. *Staffordshire County Council*), a social worker helped to lift an elderly client back into bed with the help of a neighbour who had some nursing experience. The social worker injured her back and successfully sued the employer for failing to provide her with training or some other instruction in lifting techniques. The employer's defence that the post of social worker did not normally include lifting was rejected on the ground that the employer should have ensured she was aware of the risks involved in lifting, given that she was likely to face such emergency situations.

What about pregnant workers?

Employers also have to take care in the case of pregnant workers, as manual lifting may endanger the health of the woman as well as her unborn child (see also above under the Management of Health and Safety At Work (Amendment) Regulations and under the section on maternity in Chapter 3).

Personal Protective Equipment At Work Regulations 1992

What protective clothing does your employer have to provide?

These regulations, which came into effect on 1 January 1993, cover *all* equipment which is intended to be worn by an employee and which protects her against one or more risks to her health and safety.

The regulations require the employer to provide suitable protective equipment to employees who may be exposed to a risk to their health and safety. The self-employed are also required to provide their own equipment where their health and safety may be at risk. And before choosing the equipment, the employer (or self-employed person) must carry out an assessment to make sure that it is suitable for the risk.

Does the clothing have to be in good condition?

Any equipment that the employer provides must be well maintained and kept in proper repair. Any defects should be reported to the employer. Employers are also required to make sure that the equipment fits. If it does not, then the employer is in breach of the regulations on two grounds. First, that the woman was placed at risk from the workplace hazard against which the equipment was supposed to give her protection, and second, that she was placed at risk from an injury from the ill-fitting equipment.

Provision and Use of Work Equipment Regulations 1992

What obligations do the regulations place on employers?

These regulations require employers to ensure that any work equipment provided is suitable and used safely. Employers have to assess the location in which the work equipment is to be used and take account of any risks that may arise from the particular circumstances. It must also be kept in good working order – see the case of *Stark* v. *Post Office* as a good example.

What about training and information for employees?

Those who use the work equipment must have adequate health and safety information made available to them and, where appropriate, written instructions for the use of the work equipment. They must also have received adequate training in using the equipment.

Workplace (Health, Safety and Welfare) Regulations 1992

What premises are covered by these regulations?

Effective from January 1993, these regulations aim to ensure that workplaces meet the health, safety and welfare needs of every member of the workforce, including people with disabilities. They do not, however, cover 'domestic premises', which mean a private dwelling, although they do apply to nursing homes.

Every employer must ensure that any workplace under his control complies with the regulations. Where employees work somewhere not under their employer's control (such as a private house), then the employer has no duty.

What do the regulations require the employer to do?

In essence, the regulations require that the workplace (and the equipment in it) should be maintained in good working order. For instance:

• Any enclosed workplace should be ventilated by fresh or purified air

- The temperature inside buildings should be reasonable (no less than 16 degrees), with enough thermometers provided to determine the temperature
- There should be suitable lighting
- Every workstation should be arranged so that every task can be carried out safely and comfortably, with adequate freedom of movement
- The surfaces of floors should be kept free from holes and uneven or slippery surfaces. If floors have slopes, a handrail should be provided and any holes should be repaired straight away. If this is not practicable, then the area should be protected by barriers and clearly marked
- Floors should be kept free of obstructions which could cause someone to slip, trip or fall. This is particularly important on or near empty stairs, steps, doorways and fire exits
- There must be suitable and sufficient sanitary and washing facilities provided at readily accessible places
- There must be an adequate supply of wholesome drinking water from a public or private water supply

Health and Safety (Display Screen Equipment) Regulations 1992

Who do the regulations cover?

These regulations, which also came into force on 1 January 1993, are for the protection of employees and the self-employed who regularly use display screen equipment in their normal work. Employees are covered whether they are required to work at their employer's workstation or at one provided for them at home.

Who is a 'display screen user'?

A display screen user will be someone who depends on the equipment to do their job, working at the screen for more than one hour at a time on a daily basis. These regulations will, therefore, affect many women who are employed to do clerical work, particularly the inputting of data.

What obligations do the regulations place on employers?

In brief, the regulations require that display screen users have regular breaks, preferably away from their screens. They are also entitled to eye tests at regular intervals. Basically, employers are required to assess the risks associated with display screen equipment and then do everything they can to eliminate or reduce the risk of injury.

Control of Substances Hazardous to Health (COSHH) Regulations 1994

What are substances hazardous to health?

Many women come into contact with hazardous substances in their workplaces such as cleaning materials, pesticides, hairdressing preparations or other chemicals. There are additional concerns for women because of the effect on their reproductive capacity and because they are often doubly exposed. For instance, many women cleaners may be exposed to the same chemical at home as at work.

What does the employer have to do under the regulations?

Under the COSHH regulations, employers must:

- Carry out an assessment of the risks to health from the use of substances at work by someone competent
- This should be done before anyone uses the substance
- If a risk is identified, the employer then has to eliminate it
- If that is not possible, he or she has to control the risk, perhaps by improving the ventilation system to reduce the fumes or dust. As a last resort, the employer has to provide personal protective equipment if the risk cannot be eliminated or controlled in any other way

On an ongoing basis, employers have to:

- Monitor the workplace to assess levels of harmful substances in the workplace
- Keep a record of the results of all these tests and the procedures used

Employers may also have to undertake medical surveillance of workers and provide information and training to anyone who may be exposed to the harmful substances at any time.

Working Time Regulations

Working time is a health and safety issue and the aim of the Working Time Regulations (introduced in October 1998 to implement a European directive) is to improve health and safety at work by introducing minimum rules relating to rest periods, hours and holidays. Many women work long hours – sometimes because they have more than one job or because they do shift work. Unfortunately for many women, the reason they do so is because of low pay. In those circumstances, giving you the right to reduce your hours to an average of 48 per week may not prove that helpful.

Who is Covered by the Regulations?

The regulations cover anyone who is an employee, plus a wider group doing work under other forms of contract. These could include agency and other temporary workers, as well as freelancers, although the self-employed are excluded. Also excluded are doctors in training, the armed forces and police and other sectors such as air, rail, road, sea, inland waterway and lake transport, sea fishing and other work at sea, although the reference to these excluded sectors will be removed shortly. Full application of the 48-hour week to doctors in training will take place over a four-year period.

How do you Know if you are Excluded or Included?

The scope of the current exclusions is unclear. For instance, if you are a secretary at a port, are you excluded because you work in the transport sector or included because you work in an office?

The guidance from the Department of Trade and Industry suggested that, in deciding whether the transport exclusion applied, it was the nature of the work that the individual did rather than the employer's business. It seemed likely therefore that office staff in the transport sector would be covered, but some recent decisions have thrown doubt on this. For instance, a clerical worker in a parcel delivery company has been deemed to come within the exclusion and was therefore not covered by the regulations. Further case law may throw some light on the confusion.

How is Working Time Defined under the Regulations?

The regulations define working time as time when a worker is 'working, at his employer's disposal and carrying out his activity or duties' plus any time when the worker is training. In other words, working time is when you are at the beck and call of your employer. This definition is important for obvious reasons. You need to establish whether periods of time, such as those spent on call, are counted as working time or not. The European Court of Justice has just said (*SIMAP* v. *Conselleria de Sanidad y Consumo de la Generalidad Valenciana*) that for time to be counted as working time, the worker must be at their place of work and available to work (although not necessarily working). If they are on-call, but free to pursue their own activities, that would not be counted as working time.

Equally, a lunch break spent at leisure is not working time, but if you had to have a working meeting then it would be. Travelling time to and from work would not be counted as working time, but travelling to a work meeting would count, as would doing work at home.

Given these uncertainties, it is preferable to draw up an agreement with your employer and incorporate your own definition of working time, which you can do under the regulations.

What are Workforce Agreements?

The regulations introduce a new concept of workforce, as opposed to collective, agreements. These are written agreements reached between workers (or representatives of the workforce) and their employer for a specified period, dealing with those aspects of the regulations which can be modified or excluded (see below). Collective agreements are agreements reached between trade union representatives and the employer.

What do the Regulations Say about How Long you Can Work Each Week?

A worker's average working time (including overtime) should not exceed 48 hours for each seven-day period worked, although workers can agree individually to sign an opt-out (see below for details)

No worker should suffer any disadvantage if she refuses to opt out, and anyone who has opted out can bring the agreement to an end by giving notice to the employer.

In a recent case (*Barber and others* v. *RJB Mining (UK) Ltd*), the High Court said that once workers had worked in excess of the 48-hour maximum and had not agreed to exceed those hours, they were entitled to refuse to work until their average working hours came within that limit. It also said that workers had a basic contractual right not to have to work more than an average 48-hour week. This is an important decision, because if you do not want to opt out, the courts have said that employers will be in breach of contract if they try to make you do so.

Are there Exceptions to the Limit?

This 48-hour average limitation does not apply to people with control over their working time such as senior executives, family workers and religious officials. In other words, these groups of workers are not covered at all by the 48-hour maximum and do not have to opt out. This is called the 'unmeasured working time' exception.

In addition, managers and white collar personnel – who have some of their working time predetermined (probably in their contract) by their employer, but who choose to work longer hours voluntarily in order to get the job done – are also covered by this exception. For instance, if you are required to work 35 hours per week but you regularly work 50 hours, bringing you over the average 48-hour limit, this would not represent a breach of the regulations.

Can you Ignore the Weekly Maximum Limit?

You cannot ignore the 48-hour limit, but any individual worker can agree in writing to opt out from it. The employer must keep a record of those who agree to do so, although he or she does not have to keep a record of the hours they work.

What Happens if you Have More than One Job?

If you have more than one job, your employers are supposed to make sure that you do not exceed the overall 48-hour maximum. If you are asked by one of your employers whether you are working elsewhere, you should give relevant details of all your jobs and, if you want to, sign an opt-out form with any or all of your employers if you want to work more than an average of 48 hours per week.

What Records does the Employer Have to Keep?

The employer just has to ensure that he or she has an up-to-date record of all workers who have opted out. There is no time limit for how long these records have to be kept.

How do you Work Out your Average Weekly Working Time?

Working out your average weekly working time is far from straightforward. In essence, you have to divide the number of hours you work by the number of weeks in the 'reference period', which is an arbitrary chunk of time that the year is divided into for this purpose. The reference period is usually 17 weeks unless you have agreed something different with your employer.

The calculation must also take account of periods when you are away from work because of holidays, sick leave or maternity leave plus any days when you worked in excess of the 48-hour week.

The basic formula is as follows: $\dfrac{A + B}{C}$

A is the number of hours worked in the reference period.

B is the total number of hours worked immediately *after* the reference period equal to the number of days missed *during* the reference period due to holidays, etc.

C is the number of weeks in the reference period.

Take the following example:

- You worked 17 weeks of 40 hours (eight hours a day). During the first twelve weeks of the reference period, you worked eight hours of overtime. You also took four days' holiday. All in all, therefore, you worked 16 weeks and one day (because of the four days' holiday) in that particular reference period.

  A is therefore (16 x 40) + (1 x 8) + overtime of (8 x 12) = 744
  B is therefore 4 x 8 = 32
  C is 17

  You therefore worked $\dfrac{744 + 32}{17}$ = 45.6 hours per week

Are there Similar Restrictions for Night Work?

A night worker should not work more than an *average* of eight hours in every 24-hour period. Those doing heavy work or work with special hazards should not work more than eight hours in any actual 24-hour period.

Special hazards can either be identified in a collective agreement between the union and your employer, or as part of the risk assessment carried out by the employer under the Management of Health and Safety At Work Regulations 1992 (see above).

Night workers are also restricted to working no more than an average of 48 hours per week, unless they have signed an opt-out agreement.

Can these Restrictions Be Removed?

The regulations restricting how long you can work at night can, however, be modified or excluded by a collective or workforce agreement. That means that your trade union representatives (or workforce representatives) can agree with your employer to make changes to these provisions or to get rid of them altogether.

In addition, large groups of workers are excluded altogether from restrictions on length of night working, as follows:

• Those who work far from home
• Security and caretaking staff
• Those who have to provide continuity of service or production such as hospital workers and those in residential institutions as well as dock and airport workers
• Media and postal services staff
• The utilities' workers
• Agricultural workers
• Tourism staff

In other words, the provision on night work does not apply to any of those groups of workers, such as women working in hospitals and nursing homes.

What is the Definition of a Night Worker?

A night worker is someone:

• Who works at least three hours at night on the majority of the days they work
• Who works at least three hours at night as a 'normal course', such as someone on a rotating shift pattern
• As defined in a collective or workforce agreement

In a recent case (*R* v. *Attorney General for Northern Ireland ex parte Burns*), it was established that a night worker includes someone who works nights on rotation. In this particular case, Miss Burns worked from 9 p.m. to 7 a.m. one week in every three. In other words, to come within the definition of a night worker, you do not have to be working a majority of nights in your shift cycle.

According to the regulations, night work is deemed to fall between the hours of 11 p.m. and 6 a.m. unless a different agreement is reached between the employer and his or her workforce.

What is Compensatory Rest?

Even if you are covered by an agreement which excludes or modifies how long you can work at night, you are still entitled to what is known as a period of 'compensatory rest', or, if that is not possible, to some other protection.

Presumably this means that if you are working, say, an average of ten hours per 24-hour period, you are entitled to a two-hour rest break. But don't get too excited, your employer is entitled to argue that you are getting the requisite compensatory rest during your off-duty time.

The unmeasured working time exception also applies to this provision. So if you are someone who has control over the hours you do (or at least some of them) or whose time is not monitored by your employer, then this provision will not apply to you at all.

How do you Calculate the Number of Hours Worked at Night?

Calculating night work is also a difficult business. First of all, it is the worker's normal hours of work which are relevant. That does not include any absence from work due to sickness or holidays. Nor is overtime included in the calculation, unless your contract stipulates that overtime is part of your normal working time.

Average night hours can be calculated using the following equation:

$$\frac{A}{B - C}$$

A is the number of normal working hours for that worker during the reference period.

B is the number of days during the reference period, which is usually 17 weeks but this can be extended by a collective or workforce agreement.

C is the number of hours of weekly rest to which the worker is entitled under the regulations (see below under weekly rest periods) divided by 24.

Take the following example:

- A night worker works 4 x 12 hour shifts each week during the 17-week reference period
  A is therefore 4 x 12 x 17 = 816
- The reference period is 17 weeks
  B is therefore 17 x 7 = 119
- There are 17 weekly rest periods of 24 hours to which the worker is entitled
  C is therefore $17 \times \frac{24}{24} = 17$
- The worker therefore worked as follows: $\frac{816}{119 - 17} = 8$

But remember, when calculating your hours for night work, that you still have to make sure that you are not working more than an average of 48 hours per week, unless you have opted out. So even if you do permanent nights and you have worked out that you are only doing an average of eight hours (or less) in every 24 hours, you still need to make sure that your overall weekly maximum is also within the limit.

What Records does your Employer Have to Keep?

The employer has to keep records for two years to show that the regulations on the length of night work are being complied with. The same applies to the health assessment, detailed below.

Do Employers Have to Provide Free Health Assessments for Night Workers?

Employers must give night workers the opportunity of a free health assessment before starting work and at regular intervals (probably annually). Given that it is free, a worker must not lose pay for any time lost.

A night worker is entitled to be transferred to other suitable daytime work on the advice of a doctor. The problem is that, if there is no suitable daytime work, the employer will be able to dismiss her, unless she is pregnant (see Chapter 3) or becomes unfit for night work because of a disability, in which case the employer has an obligation under the Disability Discrimination Act (see Chapter 3) to make reasonable adjustments. These might include changes to the working hours. The other problem is pay protection – the worker will want to ensure that her pay stays the same when she transfers.

This provision is not subject to any exclusions or modifications and cannot therefore be disapplied.

How Much Daily Rest is a Worker Entitled to?

Every worker is entitled to a minimum rest period of eleven consecutive hours per 24-hour period, although it is not necessary for those eleven hours to fall on the same calendar day. The same exclusions and modifications apply as for night work.

Note that if a shift worker changes shift, it may not be possible for her to take her full rest entitlement before starting her next shift in which case the entitlement to a daily rest break does not apply. Nor does it apply where her work is split up over the day, such as cleaning staff who work a morning and evening shift.

The entitlement to compensatory rest described under 'length of night work' also applies to this provision.

How Much Weekly Rest is a Worker Entitled to?

A worker is entitled to an uninterrupted rest period of not less than 24 hours in each seven-day period in addition to the daily rest break. Alternatively, the employer can provide two rest periods of 24 hours each in a 14-day period or one 48-hour rest per 14-day period. The same exclusions and modifications apply as for night work.

Note that if a shift worker changes shift, it may not be possible for her to take her full rest entitlement before starting her next shift in which case the entitlement to a weekly rest break does not apply.

The entitlement to compensatory rest described under 'length of night work' also applies to this provision.

How Much of a Rest Break is a Worker Entitled to?

Every worker is entitled to an uninterrupted rest break of no less than 20 minutes (unless something more generous has been agreed with the employer) if the working day is longer than six hours. The break should be spent away from the work station, but can be taken at any time during the working day. The same exclusions and modifications apply as for night work

The regulations do not stipulate whether the rest breaks should be paid and the issue of payment is therefore a matter for you and your employer to sort out. If your contract of employment states that they should be paid, then your employer must pay you or risk being in breach of contract.

Where the pattern of work is very monotonous, the regulations state that the worker is entitled to 'adequate rest breaks'. Quite what this means is unclear, but presumably should involve the employer giving more generous breaks than the 20 minutes stipulated in the regulations, otherwise the provision is meaningless.

What Annual Leave is the Worker Entitled to?

As from November 1999 every worker is entitled to a minimum of four weeks' *paid* annual leave per year, which can include bank and public holidays, although this may be open to challenge. To qualify, the worker has to have been employed for 13 weeks (irrespective of the number of days worked per week), but once she has got over that hurdle she is entitled to the full four weeks. The qualification period of 13 weeks is, however, being challenged as the original directive from which the regulations are taken did not stipulate any period before the worker's entitlement became effective.

When do you Start to Accrue Holiday Entitlement?

It seems from *some* tribunal decisions that the entitlement to statutory holidays accrues at the start of employment. In other words, you are entitled to four weeks' holiday from the first day of employment and do not have to wait to accrue annual leave on a week-by-week basis. Unfortunately, some other tribunals have come to the opposite conclusion. On the whole, it is worth pursuing the argument that you are entitled to the full amount of statutory holiday at the outset of your employment.

When does the Leave Year Start?

The leave year will normally start on a date to be agreed between you and your employer, but in the absence of such an agreement the regulations set a default date of 1 October. If you start work part-way through the year, then your entitlement has to be worked out on a pro rata basis.

What Pay are you Entitled to?

You are entitled to be paid a normal week's pay while on holiday, which, in the case of someone whose hours vary from week to week should be their average pay over the previous twelve weeks.

Your holiday entitlement cannot be replaced with a payment in lieu unless your employment comes to an end and you have not taken all of your entitlement by then. In other words, your employer is not allowed to deprive you of your holiday entitlement by way of a payment.

Even if you are summarily dismissed for gross misconduct and are not, therefore, entitled to any notice pay, your employer must still pay any outstanding holiday pay.

Can Statutory Holiday Entitlement Be Carried Over?

The entitlement to annual leave only applies to the leave year to which it relates – that is, it cannot be carried over. However, these stipulations only apply to statutory leave. You can agree something different with your employer for any contractual leave over and above the statutory limit to which you are entitled.

What Notice do you Have to Give?

You can reach an agreement with your employer about the notice to be given before holidays are to be taken, but in the absence of an agreement, the following applies:

- Your employer can require you to take the leave at specified times, as long as you are given notice which has to be twice as long as the period of leave. For instance, if the employer says you have to take two weeks at Christmas, then he or she will have to give you one month's notice of that
- You have to give notice to your employer if you want to take leave. Again this has to be twice the period of the leave to be taken

– so, if you want one week's holiday, give two weeks' notice. If your employer refuses to let you take the leave, he or she has to tell you within a period equivalent to the period of leave, that is, one week's notice for one week's leave

There are no modifications or exemptions from this provision.

How do you Enforce your Rights under the Working Time Regulations?

The limits in the regulations (such as the weekly working time and night work limits) will be enforced by the Health and Safety Executive and local authorities. You can either bring a problem to their attention or they may come across it when they do a spot check. If the employer still fails to comply, the Executive can bring a criminal prosecution resulting in a fine, or possibly even imprisonment for the employer.

The entitlements (rest periods, breaks and paid annual leave) will be enforced by workers bringing claims to employment tribunals. The complaint must normally be made within three months of the act or omission complained of, but may be extended if the tribunal agrees that it was not reasonably practicable to bring the complaint within that period.

What Happens if your Employer Discriminates against you?

Workers have the right not to be treated in any way disadvantageous to them in the following circumstances:

- If they refuse to go along with an employer who wants to do something in contravention of the regulations
- If they refuse to give up a right conferred on them by the regulations
- If they fail to sign up to a workforce agreement
- If they stand as a workforce representative
- If they bring proceedings against the employer to enforce a right under the regulations
- If they allege that the employer has infringed a right under the regulations

You have the right to bring a complaint to an employment tribunal within three months of the act of discrimination.

What Happens if your Employer Dismisses you?

It is automatically unfair to dismiss an employee (not a worker – see Chapter 2 for an explanation of the difference) if it is because she:

- Refused (or said she would refuse) to go along with something which her employer imposed in contravention of one of the regulations
- Refused to forgo a right conferred by the regulations
- Failed to sign a workforce agreement
- Was a workforce representative, or stood as a candidate in an election to become one, and carried out any duties in that capacity

You must lodge your claim of unfair dismissal within three months of the date of the act you are complaining about.

Violence at Work

According to a survey by the TUC (January 1999) called *Violent Times: Preventing Violence at Work*, young women between the ages of 25 and 34 were reported to be twice as likely to be attacked at work as their male counterparts. The nursing profession headed the list, with one in three subject to some kind of attack.

Can you Rely on the Health and Safety At Work Act?

Although there is no specific mention of violence in the Health and Safety At Work Act 1974, all the general duties placed on employers still apply to the risk of violence. Under the Act, employers must:

- Provide safe methods of working, safe workplaces, a safe working environment
- Provide information, instruction and training for staff

If employees are at risk from violence in their workplace and are subsequently the victim of a violent attack because their employer failed to comply with the obligations, they can sue their employer under the Health and Safety At Work Act (as well as the common law).

What about the Management of Health and Safety At Work Regulations?

In addition, the Management of Health and Safety At Work Regulations state that employers must provide a 'suitable and sufficient' assessment of any risks to the health and safety of their employees. Any assessment should cover violence at work. Although some violent incidents cannot be predicted, many are foreseeable and employers have a responsibility to identify them and seek to prevent them. Employers should:

- Identify any hazards which may affect the safety of workers arising out of the jobs they do
- Evaluate the risks arising from the hazards and plan measures to remove hazards and reduce risks
- Decide whether existing precautions are adequate or what more needs to be done
- Train and inform all workers affected
- In organisations with more than five people, write a report detailing the measures being taken to prevent violence
- Review the findings of the risk assessment periodically

Employers will have to make special arrangements for employees where hazards are identified, such as:

- Better lighting at the workplace
- Improved security, particularly for women working shifts
- Provision of mobile phones for workers on their own
- CCTV surveillance in car parks or other isolated areas
- Panic buttons for homeworkers

Working at Home and Working Alone

Homeworkers are particularly at risk from hazards (such as inadequate ventilation, lighting or seating) along with a lack of support and procedures to deal with them. The same thing applies to people who work alone, either at home or because they work outside normal hours, such as cleaners.

What Legislation Can the Homeworker Rely on?

All activities involving lone employees are covered by the Health and Safety at Work Act and by the Management of Health and Safety at Work Regulations (see above for details). Regulation 10 addresses the specific issue of people working in the premises of other organisations and the responsibility of the host employer to carry out an assessment of risks to those people. In particular, the host employer has to:

• Identify any risks and the health and safety measures in place to address them
• Provide information to those workers regarding relevant risks to their health and safety

Other regulations with implications for the lone worker and those at home include the Personal Protection Equipment at Work Regulations, the Workplace (Health, Safety and Welfare) Regulations and the Manual Handling Regulations (see above for details).

What about the Common Law?

Some homeworkers may also be able to pursue a claim for negligence under the common law, perhaps because of defective equipment supplied by the employer. You would, however, need to consult a lawyer to pursue this option.

Bullying and Harassment at Work

What are your Employer's Obligations under the Common Law?

Your employer has a general duty under the contract of employment to provide a safe system of work, safe equipment and competent employees. If you are being harassed, then he or she is likely to have breached one or more of those implied terms and you may be able to bring a claim for damages in the civil court.

In addition, you may be able to bring a claim for negligence in the civil court on the basis that you have suffered a psychological injury. This is more difficult to establish, but it may still be worth consulting a lawyer, preferably under a scheme that provides for an initial free half-hour consultation known as the Accident Legal Advice Service.

What are your Employer's Obligations under the Protection from Harassment Act 1997?

Although its original purpose was to tackle the problem of victims harassed by stalkers, the provisions of the Act are drawn widely enough to encompass any form of harassment, including that of the worker in the workplace. The Act creates two criminal offences:

- A 'low-level' offence of pursuing a course of conduct which amounts to harassment of another person and which the harasser knows or ought to have known amounts to harassment of that person, although the harasser does not have to have intended to cause the victim to feel harassed
- A 'higher-level' offence of pursuing a course of conduct which the perpetrator knows or ought to have known would cause someone else to fear (on at least two occasions) that violence was going to be used against her

The use of the term 'harassment' in the Act includes 'alarming the person or causing the person distress'. The term 'conduct' includes speech, but a 'course of conduct' must involve conduct on at least two occasions.

So if someone in your workplace uses threatening, abusive or insulting language or behaviour, then the chances are that you can make use of the Act; likewise, if someone shows you any writing or pictures which you find threatening, abusive or insulting. But remember that these are criminal offences which have to be reported to the police. You can also try to get an injunction to stop the harassment and/or sue for damages including anxiety and financial loss.

What are your Employer's Obligations under the Health and Safety at Work Act 1974?

The Act places a duty on employers to safeguard the health, safety and welfare of all employees. Bullying and harassment often have an impact on an employee's health (both physical and mental), as well as the health and safety of everyone else around them. Employers have a duty to deal with any harassment in the workplace because of the obligations placed on them under this legislation.

What about the Management of Health and Safety at Work Regulations 1992?

These regulations oblige employers to introduce an effective system to protect the health and safety of their employees. They have to assess the risks by identifying the hazards present in their undertaking and then evaluate the extent of the risks involved. Regulation 3 states that a hazard is something with the potential to cause harm, which can include any aspect of work organisation, including harassment.

What about the Employment Rights Act?

The Employment Rights Act (section 100(1)(d)) says that an employee will be deemed as unfairly dismissed if he or she left their work for health and safety reasons.

In a recent case (*Harvest Press Ltd* v. *McCaffrey*), the Employment Appeal Tribunal said that the employer had failed to ensure the safety of one of his employees as a result of harassment by another employee. The employee was therefore unfairly dismissed for having left his place of work as a result of the harassment.

Can you Use the Sex Discrimination Act and/or the Race Relations Act?

Although neither of the Acts specifically mention harassment, you can still bring a claim under the race and sex discrimination legislation.

The key to the success of your claim is to show that you have been subjected to the particular treatment because of your sex or race. But note that you do not need an *actual* comparator if the harassment is gender- or race-specific This is because, for instance, a man would not be called a 'slag' or a 'tart'.

In a ground-breaking case some years ago (*Strathclyde Regional Council* v. *Porcelli*), the Court of Session in Scotland explained that although the treatment which the applicant suffered would have been equally unpleasant if directed at a man, the fact is that sexual harassment cases are gender-specific. That is, the treatment is based on the sex of the victim and would not be used against a man. It follows that the treatment is automatically different and less favourable to a woman. The same principle applies to a racial harassment claim.

The fact that your harasser did not intend to cause you offence is irrelevant. What counts is the effect it has on you.

You can complain about behaviour which includes being shouted at or bullied, as well as overtly sexual behaviour such as indecent remarks, questions about your sex life and demands for sexual favours. In some circumstances, exposure to pin-ups or other sexually offensive material in the workplace (which includes the Internet) may amount to sexual harassment, but that is more difficult to prove.

The Sex Discrimination Act can also be used in cases of same sex discrimination, such as the case of *Gates* v. *Security Express Guards*, in which the tribunal found that harassment of a male security officer by a male supervisor amounted to sex discrimination.

Are Codes of Practice Any Help?

Both the Equal Opportunities Commission and the European Commission have produced Codes of Practice on sexual harassment which, although not legally binding, may be used by tribunals as benchmarks of good practice against which to judge employers.

Although the European code does not deal with racial harassment or harassment based on disability, the same principles are likely to apply. The Code defines sexual harassment as 'unwanted conduct of a sexual nature, or other conduct based on sex affecting the dignity of women and men at work'. This can include unwelcome physical, verbal or non-verbal conduct.

Can a Single Act Constitute Harassment?

The definition in the European Code has generated a debate about whether a single act can constitute harassment, a debate which was finally put to rest in the case of *Insitu Cleaning Co Ltd & anor* v. *Heads*, in which the employer argued that because the conduct had only taken place on one occasion, it could not be said to be unwanted until it had been rejected. The Employment Appeal Tribunal disagreed, saying that the argument amounted to a licence to harass women, on the basis that men could argue that they were just trying to find out if the conduct was unwanted or not.

How do you Make Clear that the Conduct is Unwanted?

In a recent case (*Reed and anor* v. *Stedman*), the Employment Appeal Tribunal looked at the issue of how to decide whether conduct of a sexual nature was welcome or not. It said that because it is for individuals to decide what is acceptable to them, tribunals had to assess whether the woman had made it clear that she found the conduct unwelcome.

The appeal tribunal also went on to say that tribunals will be sensitive to the difficult situations that can face women, particularly if the man is senior to her. The bottom line is that if any reasonable person would understand that the woman was rejecting the conduct of which she subsequently complained, carrying on with the conduct would be considered harassment. For instance, if the woman walked out of the room and left her harasser, that would indicate that she was rejecting the harasser's conduct.

What Claims Should you Make if you Have to Resign?

If you have to resign because you cannot bear to work in your job any longer as a result of the harassment, you may be able to claim unfair dismissal (see Chapter 6) as well as discrimination if the harassment was sufficiently serious. However, you should seek advice from your trade union, a Citizens Advice Bureau or a lawyer before doing so, as unfair dismissal claims are notoriously difficult to win. You may also want to add a claim under the Human Rights Act 1998 (see later).

What Should you Do if your Employer Fails to Deal with your Complaint?

If your employer fails to deal with your complaint of sexual harassment, that in itself may be grounds for a claim of sex discrimination (or race) depending on the circumstances.

For instance, in the recent case of *Coyne* v. *The Home Office* a woman made a complaint of sexual harassment to two different managers, neither of whom investigated because they said that she had brought it on herself. The Employment Appeal Tribunal said that the employer's failure to carry out an investigation was unlawful sex discrimination. So if your employer either does not investigate or does so very perfunctorily, remember that that failure in itself is a breach of the employer's obligation towards you.

Who Can you Claim against?

Claims of sexual and racial harassment can be brought against both the harasser and your employer, as the employer is liable for the discriminatory acts of his or her employees (see Chapter 3 for more details).

If you are an agency worker, bring your claim against the agency as well as the employer you are temporarily working for and the harasser. If you have been harassed by someone outside work – such as a driving instructor – you can still bring a claim, but it has to be in a civil court, not the employment tribunal.

Ask the Equal Opportunities Commission for help if the claim is one of sexual harassment, the Commission for Racial Equality for racial harassment.

What is the Time Limit for Bringing a Claim?

You need to bring your claim of discrimination to the employment tribunal within three months (less a day) of the date of the act of discrimination or, if there is a series of linked acts, from the date of the last act. However, sometimes it is very difficult to know whether an act is the last in a series of breaches or one which stands on its own. If in doubt, try to get your claim in within three months of one of the breaches in order to protect your rights.

What Should you Do if you are Being Harassed?

If you are being sexually or racially harassed at work, you should take the following steps:

- Make it clear to the harasser that you object to his behaviour
- Keep a record of all the incidents of harassment – date, time, place and nature of incident, as well as whether any witnesses were present
- Report the harasser to someone in authority
- If necessary, seek medical help
- Follow up the complaint – ask your employer how your complaint is going to be investigated and to be kept informed of the outcome

• Ask your employer to introduce a policy, if one does not already exist. The policy should:

1. Recognise that bullying and harassment is a problem which the employer is committed to ending
2. Be distributed to all employees, perhaps by inclusion in a works handbook
3. Identify what constitutes bullying or harassment and establish disciplinary procedures for any breaches. Clear examples of what is considered bullying and harassment should be given
4. Provide training for managers, personnel officers and, if appropriate, trade union representatives
5. Establish a complaints procedure, with clear deadlines, which ensures that the complainant can speak to a properly trained designated individual

Can you Make a Complaint under the Disability Discrimination Act 1995?

Under the Disability Discrimination Act, you have to show that you have been treated less favourably for a reason related to your disability compared with someone to whom that reason does not apply. There is a statutory defence which requires the employer to justify the less favourable treatment. However, this would (presumably) be very difficult to sustain in harassment claims. As under the race and sex discrimination legislation, there is no need to compare the treatment that would be meted out to someone to whom the disability-related reason did not apply.

According to the Code of Practice of the Act, harassing a disabled person because of their disability will 'almost always' amount to a detriment. The Code also recommends that disability-related harassment should be made a disciplinary offence and the workforce made aware that it will be taken seriously.

As with the Sex Discrimination Act and the Race Relations Act, the employer is liable for any acts of unlawful discrimination carried out by employees during the course of their employment, unless the employer can show that he or she took all practicable steps to prevent them from doing so.

Can you Use the Human Rights Act 1998?

The new Human Rights Act (effective from October 2000), based on the European Convention on Human Rights, also provides a source of legal action on the basis of the following:

- Article 3 of the Convention states that individuals have the right to be protected from 'inhuman or degrading treatment'
- Article 8 of the Convention guarantees the right to respect for private and family life
- Article 9 of the Convention guarantees the right to freedom of thought, conscience and religion

Stress at Work

If you are stressed out at work, this may be because of:

- Long hours
- Shift work
- The working environment
- The machinery and equipment you work with
- Noise pollution
- Overwork
- A monotonous job

The Health and Safety Executive has produced a Code Of Practice for employers. In its view, stress should be treated like any other health hazard, leaving the employer open to the same liabilities as if there were physical defects in the workplace.

Can you Bring a Claim under the Common Law?

Employers are under an obligation at common law to take such care for the health and safety of their employees so as not to expose them to a risk of injury.

Since the landmark case of *Walker* v. *Northumberland County Council*, the employer's legal duty of care also covers psychiatric damage, including work-related stress. In 1995, Mr Walker, a social worker, brought a claim for compensation against his employer, arguing that he had suffered a nervous breakdown as a result of pressure of work. The case succeeded, based on the argument that his employer had breached the common law duty of care by failing to take steps to reduce his workload.

However, such success is still unusual despite some recent victories. In Mr Walker's case it was only because of the very particular circumstances leading up to the case. He had been working for 15 years as a social worker with a very heavy caseload, made particularly stressful by the number of child protection cases. After his first nervous breakdown, his employers were aware of the risks to Mr Walker's health. The promise of extra help and a reduced caseload did not materialise on his return to work, and it was deemed by the court that his second breakdown was therefore foreseeable.

A junior hospital doctor also made legal history when he sued his employer for failing to protect his health and safety at work by requiring him to work over-long hours (*Johnstone* v. *Bloomsbury Health Authority*). The Court of Appeal said that his employers could not lawfully require him to work so much overtime in one week as it was reasonably foreseeable that it would damage his health, despite the fact that his contract of employment expressly required him to work a 40-hour week and to be available to work a further 48 hours' overtime on average each week.

Then in July 1999, Beverley Lancaster, a housing officer for Birmingham City Council won £67,000 for stress at work brought as a personal injury claim in the same way as any claim for physical injury arising out of an employer's negligence (*Lancaster* v. *Birmingham City Council*).

At the beginning of the year 2000, a warden at a travellers' site won over £200,000 for stress at work in an out-of-court settlement against the local council.

What Legislation Can you Rely on?

The following statutes can be relied on to bring a claim of stress at work, depending on the circumstances:

- Health and Safety at Work Act 1974 – employers have a duty to ensure that, as far as is reasonably practicable, their workplaces are safe and healthy
- Management of Health and Safety at Work Regulations 1992 – employers must assess the level of risk in the workplace and base all measures for controlling risk on this assessment
- Sex Discrimination Act – if you are being treated unfairly by, say, a male line manager who treats his female staff in an overbearing and dominating way, you could argue that such behaviour amounts to sexual harassment. The same principle would apply to the Race Relations Act
- Disability Discrimination Act 1995 – stress may turn out to be the sign of an underlying condition that would amount to a disability. Under the Act, employers are required to make reasonable adjustments to the workplace, such as reducing the employee's workload or pressures on an over-stressed employee

6
Dismissal

It will usually be obvious to both the employer and the employee when someone has been dismissed, but it is worth knowing that, in the eyes of the law, you will also have been dismissed in the following circumstances:

- When your fixed-term contract expires, but is not renewed
- When your employer refuses to let you return to work after a period of maternity absence
- When you resign because of your employer's conduct – known as 'constructive dismissal' (see below for details)

But there are a number of people who may not complain of unfair dismissal:

- Anyone who is not an employee (see section in Chapter 2 on employment status)
- Employees with less than one year's continuous service with the same employer
- Employees over 65, although this may be open to challenge
- Employees who work outside Great Britain
- Employees who resign and are not dismissed

Unfair Dismissal

Every employee has the right not to be dismissed without notice. Equally, every employer has the right to terminate an employee's contract by giving notice. But in some circumstances, the employee may want to complain that, although the employer gave the correct notice, the dismissal was unfair. To make a claim of unfair dismissal, you have to be an employee and have at least one year's continuous employment with the same employer. The law also says, however, that there will be certain circumstances when it will be fair for the employer to dismiss you.

When is it Fair to Dismiss you?

The Employment Rights Act 1996 says that there are five specific reasons that may constitute a fair reason for dismissal by the employer. These are:

- Misconduct at work
- Lack of capability (or qualifications) to do the job
- Redundancy
- A statutory requirement, such as dismissing a driver who loses her licence
- Some other substantial reason

At the employment tribunal, the onus is on the employer to establish that the dismissal falls within one of the five reasons.

How does the Tribunal Decide whether the Dismissal was Fair?

For the dismissal to be fair, the tribunal has to consider two things:

- The reason for the dismissal
- Whether the employer acted reasonably in the circumstances

Why did your Employer Dismiss you?

Before considering the second stage of the procedure, the tribunal will want to know why your employer dismissed you. The reason given must be one that was relevant at the time of dismissal. For instance, if your employer dismissed you on a whim but subsequently found out that you were engaged in large-scale fraud, he or she could not subsequently rely on that reason. However, if you serve out your notice, your employer can rely on events during the notice period to justify the decision to dismiss.

Remember that even if the tribunal decides that the reason for dismissing you falls into one of the above categories, it will still then go on to consider whether the employer was reasonable in dismissing you, given all the circumstances of the case.

What about Constructive Dismissal?

Even if you are claiming constructive dismissal (see below), your employer still has to give a reason for the dismissal even though he or she did not actually dismiss you as such. If your employer just says that there was no dismissal, but you can convince the tribunal that there was, it will then automatically be unfair. That means that the tribunal will not bother to look at whether your employer acted reasonably or not in dismissing you.

How do you Find Out the Reason for your Dismissal?

You are entitled to ask your employer for written reasons for your dismissal, which can be used in evidence at the tribunal. You have to ask for these within 14 days of the date of termination of your employment.

Was your Employer Reasonable in Dismissing you?

Even if your employer succeeds in convincing the tribunal that the dismissal was for one of the potentially fair reasons, the tribunal then has to go on to decide whether, in all the circumstances, he or she acted reasonably in dismissing you for that particular reason.

In considering this, the tribunal will take into account the following:

- The size of the employer. Basically, the bigger the employer, the more that will be expected of him or her. However, even if your employer is the corner shop, the tribunal will still expect them to follow some basic procedure
- The administrative resources available to the employer
- The employer's business needs
- The particular circumstances of the employee such as length of service or whether her performance could have been improved if the dismissal was for capability

The tribunal will also look at whether the employer dealt fairly with the employee. For instance, if you can show that other employees were dealt with more leniently than you in similar circumstances, this could result in a finding of unfair dismissal.

Was the Internal Procedure Fair?

Procedural fairness is an integral part of the reasonableness test.

In the famous case of *Polkey* v. *AE Dayton Services*, the House of Lords said that the following procedural steps should be followed by employers if the dismissals were to be fair:

- In a case of capability, the employee must be given a fair warning and a chance to improve (see section on sickness in Chapter 4 for more details)
- In a case of misconduct, employers must investigate fully and fairly and hear what the employee has to say in mitigation or explanation
- In a case of redundancy, employers must give a warning and consult affected employees, adopt a fair basis for selection and take reasonable steps to re-deploy affected employees (see section below for more details)

The court also ruled that, if there was a fundamental flaw in the employer's procedure, the dismissal may well be unfair, although not automatically so. However, the court also said that, in exceptional cases, if the employer could show that it would have been completely futile to follow a proper procedure, then it might be reasonable to ignore it.

Should you Have a Right of Appeal?

Every disciplinary procedure should provide a right of appeal. If you are refused the right to appeal by your employer, then the chances are that your dismissal will be unfair. If you have a contractual right to appeal which has been withheld by your employer, then it is almost certain to result in a finding of unfair dismissal. In those circumstances, there would also be a breach of contract.

ACAS has produced a Code of Practice on disciplinary practice and procedures which tribunals often take into account when deciding whether an employer has acted fairly. A copy of the booklet can be obtained from ACAS.

What Happens if you do Not Make Use of the Internal Procedure?

If you have been made aware of an internal disciplinary procedure and you fail to make use of it, your compensation (if you are successful in your claim) will be reduced by two weeks' pay as a result. Conversely, if your employer prevented you from making use of the appeal procedure, your compensation will be increased by a maximum of two weeks' pay.

What are the Automatically Unfair Reasons for Dismissal?

There are a number of dismissals which are automatically unfair, for which you do not need one year's service with your employer. In addition, the tribunal does not have to consider the reasonableness of the dismissal. If you can show that the dismissal was for one of the following reasons, then the tribunal will deem it automatically unfair and the issue of reasonableness does not apply:

- Dismissal in connection with trade union membership (or non-membership) or activities
- Dismissal for a reason connected with pregnancy
- Dismissal for a health and safety reason
- Dismissal of an employee representative in connection with her duties in that capacity
- Dismissal for asserting a statutory right such as asking for time off for ante-natal care
- Dismissal where there is a transfer of an undertaking
- Dismissal for refusing to work on a Sunday
- Dismissal in connection with the part-time work regulations, parental leave rights, national minimum wage, the working time regulations, a public interest disclosure or selection for redundancy for one of the above reasons

Constructive Dismissal

If an employee resigns in response to a significant and fundamental breach of the employment contract by the employer, this is known as a constructive dismissal. It is, however, difficult to prove and employees should think carefully before resigning and claiming that there has been a constructive unfair dismissal. In order to bring a claim, the employee needs to have at least one year's continuous service with the same employer.

What do you Have to Prove for Constructive Dismissal?

Not every breach of contract will entitle an employee to claim constructive dismissal. She has to prove a number of points:

- First of all, there has to be a fundamental breach. In other words, the employer must have breached a clause of the contract which is so integral to it that it appears that he or she no longer intends to be bound by the contract. For example, a reduction in pay, a change in an employee's status, changes in hours of work or place of work (unless the contract has an express clause to the contrary), might constitute such a fundamental breach
- Next, the employee has to make sure that she resigns in response to that fundamental breach and not for any other reason, otherwise the claim will not succeed. It is helpful, therefore, to give written reasons when you leave which can be used in evidence at the tribunal hearing
- Finally, for a constructive dismissal claim to have any hope of success, the employee must resign promptly, because any delay may be taken by the tribunal as acceptance of the employer's conduct. How long an employee can afford to delay depends on the facts of each case, but if the employee can point to specific circumstances, this may justify a longer delay than would otherwise have been accepted

In *Western Excavating* v. *Sharp*, Lord Denning explained that the employee 'must make up his mind soon after the conduct of which he complained; for if he continues for any length of time without leaving, he will lose his right to treat himself as discharged'.

Should I Resign and Claim Constructive Dismissal?

Before taking such a drastic step, take advice from your trade union or an employment lawyer. Constructive dismissal claims are notoriously difficult to win and, although you may feel yours is a cast iron case, you risk losing your job and ending up with no compensation if you act in haste.

One alternative to resigning is to work under protest under the new terms (see Chapter 4 for more details) and claim unfair dismissal from the original contract. You may need help from your trade union, a lawyer or a Citizens Advice Bureau for this.

What is the Time Limit for Lodging a Constructive Dismissal Claim?

As with unfair dismissal, a claim must be lodged within three months (less one day) of the effective date of termination (see later). In claims of constructive dismissal, this is problematic to work out but it is likely to be the date on which you walked off the job.

Wrongful Dismissal

What is Wrongful Dismissal?

Unlike unfair dismissal, which is a statutory right, wrongful dismissal is a contractual right. It comes about when an employer terminates the employment contract contrary to the terms contained in it. This would happen if, for instance, the employer failed to give the correct notice or failed to follow the contractual disciplinary procedure.

What Claim Should you Make if you are Wrongfully Dismissed?

A wrongfully dismissed employee should make a claim for breach of contract, for which the remedy is an award of damages.

You can bring the claim in an employment tribunal, a county court or the High Court. However, the employment tribunal can only make a maximum award of £25,000. The employee has six years from the date of the alleged breach to bring proceedings in the county court or High Court and three months (less one day) from the effective date of termination in the employment tribunal.

What if your Employer Fails to Give Proper Notice?

Where the breach is the failure to give proper notice, compensation will usually be loss of earnings for the notice period, subject to mitigation. This just means that the employee is expected to take all reasonable steps to reduce the size of the claim by seeking alternative employment and claiming any benefit due. This money is then set off against the claim.

What if the Breach is a Failure to Follow the Disciplinary Procedure?

Where the breach is the failure to follow a contractual disciplinary procedure, the amount of compensation varies. In some cases, it may be wages for the time the employer would have taken to exhaust the procedure, had it been followed. It is, however, unlikely that you can claim compensation on the basis that you would not have been dismissed had the employer followed the correct procedure.

> In a recent case (*Janciuk* v. *Winerite Ltd*), Mr Janciuk was summarily dismissed by the respondent and given two weeks' pay in lieu of notice. Mr Janciuk claimed he was contractually entitled to the benefit of the disciplinary procedure, which, if it had been followed, might have meant he would not have been dismissed. He argued that compensation for this failure should have been included in his damages. The Employment Appeal Tribunal said that Mr Janciuk was not entitled to be compensated for the loss of the chance to go through a disciplinary procedure in the hope that he might not have been dismissed.

Summary Dismissal

What is Summary Dismissal?

This is when your employer dismisses you on the spot without giving you notice. Usually this happens if you have committed an act of gross misconduct. There are no definitive rules as to what constitutes gross misconduct, but it is usually something which is so serious that it undermines the contract you have with your employer, such as being drunk at work, fighting at work or stealing from your employer. Some contracts set out a list of misdemeanours that constitute gross misconduct.

Does your Employer Still Have to Conduct an Investigation?

Although your employer can dismiss you without notice, that is not the same as saying that he or she does not have to have an investigation into the matter. Employers still have to follow their own internal disciplinary procedures (which usually give examples of behaviour that constitutes gross misconduct) and give you a chance to put your side of the story. However, if you are ultimately found guilty of gross misconduct, you can then be dismissed without notice. That does not stop you from claiming unfair dismissal, if you have been working for the employer for a year or more.

Redundancy

Redundancy is one of the potentially fair reasons for dismissal. To challenge the 'fairness' of a redundancy decision, you would need, therefore, to look at the circumstances surrounding the redundancy. For instance, you would need to consider:

- Whether there is a genuine redundancy situation (see below)
- What selection criteria were used to decide who would be made redundant (see below)
- What pool was used to determine who should be made redundant (see below)
- The sex and marital status and jobs of those selected for redundancy as opposed to those who were not
- What reasons you were given as to why you were chosen

What Constitutes a Redundancy?

Dismissal by reason of redundancy occurs if the reason, or the main reason, for the dismissal falls into one of the following situations:

- There has been closure of the business as a whole
- There has been closure of the particular workplace where the employee worked
- There has been a reduction in the size of the workforce needed for doing work of a particular kind

What do you Have to Prove to Challenge a Redundancy Decision?

To bring a claim for unfair dismissal where the reason for dismissal is redundancy, you would have to show that:

- That there was no general redundancy situation, or
- That the employer failed to consult about the redundancy, or
- That you were unfairly selected, or
- That your employer unreasonably failed to offer alternative employment, or
- That the method of implementing the redundancies had not been carried out reasonably

The vast majority of cases are fought on the basis of unfair selection and/or reasonableness (see below).

What do you Do if the Reason Given is Closure of the Business?

The answer is that it depends. If your employer has completely shut down the business, you will be redundant. However, it may be that your employer is just engaged in changing the type of business carried out at the workplace. For instance, closing a steak house for refurbishment and reopening it a month later as a brasserie will not constitute closure of a business. In those circumstances, you can argue that there was no true redundancy situation.

If the employer transfers the business to a new owner, the question of redundancy depends on whether the transfer is covered by the special rules contained in the Transfer of Undertakings (Protection of Employment) Regulations 1981. If there is a transfer, then all existing employees become employees of the new owner and there is no redundancy situation. Unfortunately, it is very difficult to know when a transfer comes under these very complicated regulations. To find out you would have to seek specialist advice – try your trade union or a specialist employer lawyer.

What if your Employer Has Closed the Place where you Worked?

If your employer closes down the workplace where you work, then you will be redundant, even if he or she continues the business elsewhere. There is usually no problem in identifying where someone works – in most cases, it is where she reports every day – but if the contract contains a mobility clause, it may be more difficult.

Take the case of the silver service waitresses in *High Table Ltd* v. *Horst & ors* who were made redundant because fewer staff were needed where they had been working. The waitresses argued that although they had only worked in one place, their employment contracts contained a mobility clause which allowed the employer to relocate them to work elsewhere. The court disagreed and said that, irrespective of the mobility clause, what mattered was where they had been working in reality.

In effect, to work out whether you are genuinely redundant, you have to look at where you were working, irrespective of whether or not you had a mobility clause. That means that if you were working mainly in one place which has closed down, then the redundancy is likely to be fair. If, on the other hand, the employer has been in the habit of moving you from one workplace to another, then it will be much harder for him or her to argue that you are now redundant.

What if the Reason is a Diminishing Need for Employees?

This provision covers the situation where the employer needs fewer employees to carry out specific work.

For instance, in a recent case (*Murray & anor* v. *Foyle Meats Ltd*), the employer decided to reduce the number of people working in the slaughter hall because of a decline in business. Mr Murray was selected for redundancy but objected on the basis that, although he normally worked in that part of the plant, his contract stated that he could be required to work in any part of the factory and occasionally did so. However, the House of Lords said that what the contract said was irrelevant. What mattered was whether the redundancy was due to the need to reduce the number of employees doing work of a particular kind.

Again, the outcome for employees is reasonably straightforward. If your employer can show that he or she needs fewer employees to do work of a particular kind (and that was the work you did) and dismisses you as a result, the dismissal is very likely to be fair by reason of redundancy.

Can Employers 'Bump' Employees into Redundancy?

The practice of 'bumping' occurs where one employee's job has become surplus to requirements, but another employee is dismissed instead. For instance, an employer needs fewer drivers, but sacks a packer and givers the packer's job to the driver. This can also be a fair dismissal by reason of redundancy.

What Pay are you Entitled to on Redundancy?

Under the Employment Rights Act, an employee dismissed on the grounds of redundancy will be entitled to redundancy pay if:

- She has two or more years' continuous service with the same employer, since the age of 18
- She is below normal retirement age

For each full year of continuous employment, up to a maximum of 20, an employee is entitled to the following:

- From age 18 to 21 – half a week's pay per year of service
- From age 22 to 40 – one week's pay per year of service
- From age 41 to 64 – one and a half weeks' pay per year of service

There is a limit to the basic weekly pay which can be claimed, which is currently set at £230, but which is updated every year.

You may, of course, be entitled to a more generous package under the terms of your contract, so it worth checking it to see what you may be owed.

What is your Entitlement if you Go Part Time, Having Worked Full Time?

This may be hard to believe, but your redundancy entitlement will be calculated on the hours being worked when you are made redundant. In other words, if for ten years, you worked full time, but then went part time for six months and were made redundant, the redundancy calculation in made on the basis of the part-time hours.

This anomalous situation has just been upheld by the House of Lords (no less) in the case of *Barry* v. *Midland Bank*. The applicant worked for the bank full time for eleven years and, after maternity leave, returned to work part time until she was made redundant three years later. Her severance pay was calculated on the final pay she was earning at the date of termination, thus ignoring her full-time service. She claimed that this amounted to indirect discrimination against women, but for some reason, the House of Lords did not agree.

There is, however, a chance that the part-time workers regulations will be of some help in this situation.

Can you Lose your Right to a Redundancy Payment?

The right to claim a redundancy payment can be lost if:

- The employee is offered her old job back, or a suitable alternative, which is unreasonably refused (see later)
- The employee is dismissed for gross misconduct during the redundancy notice
- The employee resigns before the end of the notice period

If the employer fails to make a redundancy payment, the redundant employee should lodge a claim with the employment tribunal office within six months of the dismissal taking effect.

Does your Employer Have to Consult Collectively in the Event of Redundancy?

Employers are under a statutory duty to inform and consult the recognised trade union or, where there is no union, elected representatives if more than 20 employees *at one establishment* are going to be made redundant within a period of 90 days or less. Consultation must take place with the representatives of all employees who may be affected by the redundancies, not just those whom the employer proposes to make redundant.

The regulations state that consultation must begin with the representatives:

- 'In good time', or at least 90 days before the first dismissal if there are to be 100 or more redundancies
- Otherwise, consultation has to start 30 days before the first dismissal

The employer has to provide the representatives (whether trade union or otherwise) with the following information in writing:

- The reasons for the proposals
- The numbers and descriptions of employees to be dismissed
- The total number of employees who fit that description at the workplace in question
- The proposed method of selection
- The proposed method of carrying out the dismissals and over what period of time
- The proposed method of calculating the amount of contractual redundancy payments to be made

The aim of the consultation is to reach agreement with the representatives and must look at ways of:

- Avoiding the dismissals, for example, by natural wastage or reducing overtime
- Reducing the numbers of employees to be dismissed
- Mitigating the consequences of the dismissals

The consultation must begin before the employer starts sending out dismissal notices and the union (or other) representatives must have time to consider the proposals properly, the aim being to try to ensure the exercise is not a sham.

What Can you Do if your Employer Fails to Consult?

If the employer fails to consult properly, the employees concerned can make a claim to a tribunal and ask for compensation, known as a protective award.

What is an 'Establishment' under Collective Consultation?

Needless to say, no one is entirely clear as to what an 'establishment' might be, although the European Court of Justice has said that it is the unit where employees are assigned. It will generally be in the employee's best interests to argue that as many units as possible are part of one establishment so as to trigger the collective consultation requirements, but this may be difficult using the ECJ definition.

For instance, in one case (*Barratt Developments (Bradford) Ltd* v. *UCATT*), the Employment Appeal Tribunal said that 14 house-building sites were one establishment, on the basis that each had a temporary shed linked by telephone to one headquarters.

On the other hand, in another case, a tribunal held that five shoe factories, three of which were within one mile of head office, the other two being 30 miles away, were separate establishments. What was important was the geographical separation and managerial independence of the factories, as was the fact that they were permanent, not temporary sites.

Does the Employer also Have to Consult Individually?

Just because the employer has consulted collectively does not mean he or she is released from the obligation to consult with individual employees, although individual consultation is not an absolute prerequisite in every case. However, the bigger the employer, the more that will be expected by a tribunal in terms of consultation with individual employees. The employer also has to act reasonably in terms of an internal procedure if the dismissal is to be fair.

It is up to the tribunals to decide whether the employee was consulted properly, but for the dismissal to be fair the employer needs to have:

- Consulted when the proposals were at a formative stage
- Provided adequate information to the employee
- Provided adequate time in which to respond
- Given serious consideration to any response by the employee

In *Polkey* v. *AE Dayton Services* (see above), the House of Lords made it clear that an employer's failure to warn and consult employees in a redundancy situation is likely to result in an unfair dismissal. It is only if the employer can show that consultation would have been pointless that he or she can get round the obligation to consult an individual, and this is rare.

The employee should be given the chance to discuss any personal factors which might influence the employer's decision to dismiss as well as the possibility of suitable, alternative employment.

Is your Employer Obliged to Find Suitable Alternative Employment?

If your employer fails to take reasonable steps to find alternative employment for you, the dismissal may be unfair. However, your employer does not have to create a new job for you – he or she just has to take reasonable steps to find some alternative that would be suitable. If you work in one of a group of companies, for instance, your employer should also look in those associated companies to see if there is any suitable work for you.

What about the Statutory Trial Period?

If you accept further employment with your employer (or an associated one) and the terms do not differ from the old employment, then there is no dismissal. But if the terms are different, you are entitled to a statutory trial period of at least four weeks in the new job, but without prejudicing your redundancy rights. If you find at any time during that period that the job does not suit you, you can give notice of termination and the original redundancy dismissal stands. But if neither side terminates during the trial period, then the original redundancy vanishes for good.

Your employer cannot deny you the right to the statutory trial period and if he or she tries to do so, you can bring a claim of unfair dismissal.

What about Paid Time Off to Look for Other Work?

An employee who has received notice of dismissal has the right to ask her employer for paid time off during working hours either to look for new employment or to make arrangements for training for future employment. The amount of time off to which you are entitled is probably no more than a couple of days – the test is what is reasonable in the circumstances. If your employer refuses to let you have the time off, you can complain to an employment tribunal.

How Should your Employer Go about Making Redundancies?

Even though redundancy is a potentially fair reason for dismissal, you may still be able to bring a claim for unfair dismissal if your employer acts unreasonably, say, in terms of the selection criteria he or she adopts. These must be objectively chosen and fairly applied.

To work out whether a redundancy is likely to be considered reasonable or not by a tribunal, look at all of the following:

- The pool for selection – that is, the group of employees from which the redundancies were made
- The selection criteria used to pick them
- The way in which the criteria were applied

How did your Employer Decide on the Pool for Selection?

If your employer has not even thought about what group of employees the redundancies will come from but just picks out individuals at random, the dismissal is very likely to be unfair, unless there are extenuating circumstances. Your employer needs, therefore, to begin the process by defining the appropriate pool from which to select the redundant workers.

First of all, if there is an agreement with your employer – perhaps through the trade union – which specifies the pool, your employer needs to have a good reason for not sticking to it. If there is no such agreement, it is clear that employers will have a lot more flexibility, but they still need to show that they thought about the problem, that they acted from genuine motives and that they consulted. However, there are limits to the flexibility. For instance, employers cannot just exclude certain employees from the pool – they need to have a reason for doing so.

What Selection Criteria Should your Employer Use?

Even if the selection pool is reasonable, the redundancies may still be unfair as a result of the selection criteria applied. These must be objective and may include the following:

- Last in, first out (LIFO) – although length of service is still commonly used by employers, it may be indirectly discriminatory against women because of breaks of service due to childbirth. If LIFO affects more women than men, it may be worth considering a challenge (see Chapter 3 for a detailed explanation of indirect discrimination)
- Skill and knowledge – to be objective criteria, they have to be assessed objectively. If your employer is using vague or ambiguous terms such as 'attitude to work', these may not be objective enough

- Attendance records – this should not be the sole criterion for redundancy, not least because one long (but legitimate) period of absence may distort an employee's otherwise unblemished record. In addition, the period over which attendance is assessed needs to be substantial to avoid distortions. Other blips can arise if attendance and productivity are linked. In addition, although your employer does not have to take into account why you were absent, this may be shown to be discriminatory particularly for the disabled. Note that employers cannot include breaks for maternity leave in calculating absence
- Age – the government's Code of Practice on age recommends that age should not be used as the sole criterion when selecting for redundancy. If your employer dismisses employees who have reached the normal retirement age, then, in theory, they cannot bring a claim but recent cases have thrown this in doubt
- Health – it is reasonable to take someone's health record into account in the selection process, but your employer should consult the employees concerned and consider offering them alternative employment, if any exists. If they do not, then the ensuing dismissal is likely to be unfair and discriminatory

Local trade union officials or employee representatives are not entitled to any special treatment in a redundancy situation. If the selection criteria are applied objectively, they are treated like anybody else.

How Can you Find Out if your Assessment was Carried Out Fairly?

If you believe that you have been treated unfairly in the assessment process, you may want to check the accuracy of your employer's markings. Unfortunately, this may be difficult as your employer just has to show that the selection criteria were fair and reasonably applied. However, if your employer cannot explain how any of the marks were allocated, then the tribunal may look at whether the selection criteria have been fairly applied.

You are also entitled to see your own assessments at the consultation stage, giving you a chance to contest your selection. Generally, you will not be allowed to see the assessments of others who have been retained unless you can point to a particular employee who you claim should have been selected instead of you.

Can you Bring a Claim on the Basis that your Dismissal was Discriminatory?

If you can show that your employer's selection criteria or the way in which they were applied discriminate on the grounds of sex, race or disability, then your dismissal will be contrary to the relevant discrimination legislation as well as being unfair. Compensation is unlimited in discrimination claims, but is restricted to £50,000 in unfair dismissal complaints.

- Sex and race – it is unlikely that any selection criteria would discriminate directly on the grounds of sex or race, but they may well discriminate indirectly (see Chapter 3 for an explanation of direct and indirect discrimination). For instance, if your employer selects part-timers for redundancy, this is likely to be indirectly discriminatory against women if far more women than men work part time in your organisation. Or if only senior staff are retained, this would also be indirectly discriminatory against women if fewer women than men were in senior positions. But remember that if the employer can objectively justify their criteria, they will have a defence to an indirect discrimination claim
- Disability – if your employer uses the fact of your disability to your disadvantage, he or she will have discriminated against you, unless it can be justified

For instance, in the case of *British Sugar* v. *Kirker*, the applicant, who was partially sighted, was selected for redundancy after 20 years' service. In his assessment, Mr Kirker's employer had given him no marks for performance and potential. The tribunal said that he had not been marked objectively and that his employer's attitude to his disability had coloured their judgement of him. He received damages of just over £160,000.

- Age – although there is no particular law tackling age discrimination (see Chapter 3), the government has issued a voluntary code of practice which says that a person's age should not be the sole criterion in a redundancy selection exercise.

What if you are Dismissed for Reasons Connected with your Pregnancy?

It is automatically unfair to select a woman for redundancy because she is pregnant, has given birth or taken maternity leave. This right applies irrespective of length of service or hours of work. Any woman made redundant during her maternity leave is entitled to be offered suitable, alternative work. Although your employer has a general obligation to offer alternative work before dismissing employees, women on maternity leave must be given the first offer of any vacancy. If your employer fails to do so, then you should make a claim of sex discrimination and unfair dismissal.

In the recent case of *McGuigan* v. *T G Baynes & Sons*, Ms McGuigan, a legal executive with a firm of solicitors, was made redundant while on maternity leave without any consultation. She was subsequently told that she was selected rather than the two men in the department because, as solicitors, they could become partners in the firm. She was given the lowest marks in an assessment exercise which included a poor mark for 'attitude to work', reflecting recent criticisms she had made of the firm's equal opportunities policy.

The Employment Appeal Tribunal found that she had been directly discriminated against and had also been victimised. It said that had she not been on maternity leave she would have been consulted.

It is also a form of sex discrimination if your employer takes into account any pregnancy-related absences when considering whom to make redundant. However, the only absences that can be discounted are those during the pregnancy or the maternity leave. Once the maternity leave has ended, the woman then has to be treated in the same way as anyone else.

Take the case of *Healy* v. *William B Morrison & Son Ltd* in which the applicant was made redundant two weeks after her maternity leave came to an end, although she was off work with post-natal depression. She had also had time off during the pregnancy. A man on long-term sick leave was kept on by the employers.

The appeal tribunal said that the employers could not take into account the periods of absence taken off by the woman during her pregnancy. This meant that the woman had to be treated the same as a man who had only had two weeks off work. As a result, the tribunal found that she had been dismissed due to her pregnancy and had been discriminated against on the ground of her sex.

The Notice Period

Can you Withdraw your Notice?

Once you have given notice to quit (or been given notice by your employer), neither of you can unilaterally withdraw it. So if you hand in your notice and then change your mind, you need your employer's agreement to make that change of heart effective.

What about Summary Dismissal during the Notice Period?

The fact that the notice cannot be withdrawn unilaterally does not alter the right of either party to terminate the contract summarily (see above) during the notice period.

For instance, if you give one month's notice of termination and the next day the employer cuts your pay or demotes you, then you still have the right to leave immediately and claim constructive dismissal (see above for an explanation); or if you commit an act of gross misconduct such as theft, your employer can dismiss you without notice (see above).

If you want to leave before the end of the notice period, you will need the agreement of your employer, unless, as explained above, he or she behaves in such a way that justifies your immediate exit.

What about Notice in the Event of Redundancy?

In redundancy situations, employers may try to give as much notice as possible of impending dismissals which may mean that you get a warning of an impending redundancy without an actual date of termination. It is worth knowing that if you find another job before you get the formal notice of dismissal, you will be treated by the courts as though you left of your own free will and therefore forfeit any right to a redundancy payment.

Are you Entitled to a Guaranteed Minimum Pay during the Notice Period?

You may also be entitled to a guaranteed minimum pay during your notice period, but only if you are entitled to the statutory minimum period of notice (see Chapter 4). If your contractual notice period is longer than the statutory entitlement by a week or more, then the guaranteed pay provisions do not apply.

In essence, the law says that if you are:

- Ready and willing to work, but there is no work; or
- You cannot work because of sickness or injury; or
- You are away from work because of pregnancy or childbirth; or
- You are on holiday

then you must receive your minimum average hourly rate of pay during the notice period. To work out what it should be, divide your normal week's pay by the normal weekly hours of work.

How does Guaranteed Minimum Pay Work in Practice?

Consider the following example. Two employees, X and Y, have a *contractual* notice period of one month. X has three years' service which means she is entitled to three weeks' *statutory* notice and Y has five, giving her five weeks' entitlement under statute. They are put on a three-day week and then both are made redundant. X's notice period under contract is one week more than her entitlement under statute and she cannot therefore benefit from the minimum pay provisions. But Y is entitled to be paid her minimum wage throughout the notice period, which means she will be paid on the basis of a five-day, not a three-day, week.

Do you Have to Work Out your Notice Period?

Generally speaking, you have no right to insist on working out your notice leave, nor do you have a legal right to leave and claim payment in lieu of notice unless the contract says so. However, the courts have indicated that, particularly where the notice periods are very long, individuals may have a legitimate complaint if they would suffer a deterioration in skills and/or reputation by sitting at home for a long time.

Effective Date of Termination (EDT)

What is the EDT?

This may seem an obvious question, but there is plenty of case law which says otherwise. Basically, the EDT is the date when the contract comes to an end. If notice is given by one side or the other (whether orally or in writing), then the EDT will be the end of the notice period – not the date when the notice was given. If notice is not given, then the date of termination is the date when the employee ceases to work or is summarily dismissed. If the employee is on a fixed-term contract which expires without being renewed, then the date of termination is the date when the contract ended. If the employee is given pay in lieu, then the EDT is the date of the dismissal.

What Happens if you Get Pay in Lieu of Notice?

If you are given a payment in lieu of working out your notice, for instance, if you are put on garden leave, then your EDT is the date when the notional notice period expires. However, if you are given a payment to end the contract there and then, the EDT is your last day at work. Although the distinction may seem an obscure legal one, it matters for calculating when a claim has to be submitted to a tribunal. A useful rule of thumb is to present the claim within three months of the last day actually worked.

What is the EDT if you are Given Incorrect Notice?

If your employer gives you notice which is less than that to which you are entitled under statute, then the EDT must be extended to the date when the correct notice period expires.

Whistleblowing

What does Whistleblowing Involve?

Generally, workplace whistleblowing involves disclosures by employees (or former employees) of wrongdoing such as fraud, malpractice, breach of health and safety laws or any other illegal act, either on the part of management or fellow employees. Until recently, workers in the UK had no specific statutory protection if they were dismissed by their employer, following such a disclosure.

What does the Public Interest Disclosure Act 1998 Do?

The Public Interest Disclosure Act 1998 has now introduced special protection for workers wanting to 'blow the whistle' on their employer to a third party. It does not, however, give a general right of protection to all whistleblowers, but instead requires disclosures to be made through appropriate channels. In addition, the worker will only be protected if the disclosure is one covered by the provisions.

Who is Covered?

The Act covers most individuals in the workplace. For instance:

- Employees (including apprentices)
- Agency workers
- Homeworkers
- NHS doctors, dentists and pharmacists
- Trainees on vocational schemes
- Crown servants
- The self-employed who work personally on a contract, but not genuinely self-employed professionals such as accountants or those in business on their own account

For some reason, it excludes voluntary workers along with police officers and members of the armed forces.

Are there Any Limits on the Disclosures that are Protected?

The Act only applies to a worker who discloses information about a malpractice involving one of the following:

- A crime
- A breach of an individual's legal obligations
- A miscarriage of justice
- A danger to health and safety
- Damage to the environment
- Concealment of information about any of the above

The standard to be used is a subjective one. In other words, the worker does not have to show that a crime has been committed, only that she has reasonable grounds to believe that this is the case. But the disclosure will not be a protected one under the Act if the worker herself commits an offence by virtue of making it. Likewise, if it is a disclosure protected by legal privilege.

What Procedure do you Have to Follow?

To qualify for protection, the worker has to follow one of the six specified methods of disclosure:

- Disclosure to employer made in good faith – the Act encourages the worker to raise the matter internally with her employer, particularly where there is an internal procedure. This would cover the situation where the employer has a specific whistleblowing procedure and disclosure is allowed to a third party such as external auditors or a retired non-executive director
- Disclosure to legal adviser – this covers making a disclosure in the course of obtaining legal advice
- Disclosure to a Minister of the Crown made in good faith – the disclosure is also protected if the worker's employer is an individual appointed by a Minister of the Crown, or a body whose members are appointed by a Minister
- Disclosure to a prescribed person – that is, an outside body or appropriate regulatory body prescribed by the Secretary of State in the Public Interest Disclosure (Prescribed Persons) Order 1999 SI 1999/1549. For an external disclosure to be protected, the worker must show that she was making it in good faith and that the information disclosed was true
- Disclosure in other cases – to obtain protection in any other circumstances than those described above, the worker must show that she made the disclosure in good faith, that she has a reasonable belief that the information disclosed is true and that she will not make a personal gain from the disclosure. She must also believe that she would be subjected to a detriment if she was to make the disclosure to her employer and that the evidence is likely to be destroyed if she was to do so
- Disclosure of 'exceptionally serious' breaches – the worker has to show that she made the disclosure in good faith; that she believes the information is true; that she will not make a personal gain from the disclosure; that it is exceptionally serious; and that it is reasonable for her to make the disclosure, given the circumstances

What are your Rights if your Employer Victimises you?

A worker has the right not to be treated badly by her employer just because she made a protected disclosure. Under the Act, anyone victimised at work for making a protected disclosure would receive compensation which is just and equitable in the light of her loss. The award can be reduced where the worker fails to mitigate her loss or was at fault. No minimum or maximum levels apply in these cases.

You should lodge your claim for victimisation within three months (less one day) of the alleged act.

What are your Rights if your Employer Dismisses you?

You can claim automatically unfair dismissal if you are an employee (as opposed to a worker) if the main reason is that you made a protected disclosure. No service qualification is required to qualify for this provision, nor if you are selected for redundancy. Even if you are above normal retirement age, you will still be protected by this provision. Your claim should be made within three months (less a day) of the effective date of termination.

What does the Act Say about Gagging Clauses?

The Act also makes provision for outlawing gagging clauses. It says that any provision in an agreement which tries to prevent a worker from making a protected disclosure will be void. However, it is not clear just how far-reaching the effect of the provision will be. For instance, it is unclear whether it could override a secrecy clause in a compromise or ACAS agreement for settling an unfair dismissal claim.

What Other Statutory Protection Exists for Whistleblowers?

In addition, claims can be made under the Equal Pay Act 1970, the Sex Discrimination Act 1975, the Race Relations Act 1976 or the Disability Discrimination Act 1995 as well as a number of other statutes which allow for a measure of protection, as follows:

• Under the Employment Rights Act 1996, employees are given protection against action short of dismissal and/or dismissal by their employers in cases where they take action to avert dangers to health and safety. Designated health and safety representatives are also protected in performing their statutory health and safety functions, and an employee other than an official representative is also protected where she brings circumstances to the employer's attention which she reasonably believes are harmful to health and safety

- Where an employee is dismissed for bringing proceedings to enforce a statutory right or for asserting that the employer had infringed such a right, she will be deemed to have been automatically unfairly dismissed
- The victimisation provisions in the Race Relations Act 1976, the Sex Discrimination Act 1975 and the Disability Discrimination Act 1995 provide some protection for employees who raise concerns regarding matters covered by those Acts. But there are problems, notably the requirement to prove a causal link between the less favourable treatment and the 'protected' activity (see Chapter 3 for an explanation of victimisation)
- Provided she has one year's continuous employment with the same employer, an employee dismissed for whistleblowing can bring a claim for unfair dismissal

7
Post-employment Problems

Claims and Representation

What Claims Can Be Heard by Tribunals?

The procedure for lodging a claim at an employment tribunal is more or less the same, irrespective of the type of claim you want to make. Tribunals will hear the following complaints:

- Redundancy payments
- Discrimination
- Unfair dismissal
- Breach of contract (up to £25,000)
- Deductions from wages
- Miscellaneous employment protection rights such as time off for ante-natal care, written statement of reasons for dismissal

There are some (such as breach of contract) claims which you can bring in either the employment tribunal or the county court when your employment terminates, but if the claim is likely to be for £25,000 or more, then you have to bring it in the county court.

Do you Need Someone to Represent you?

You also need to consider whether you want someone to represent you. If you are in a union or if the local Citizens Advice Bureau is supporting you, then so much the better. Occasionally the Equal Opportunities Commission or Commission for Racial Equality will offer legal support, but this is usually only in circumstances where the case would set a precedent or have an impact on a lot of other women. There is, of course, no harm in asking.

A word of warning. If someone is representing you, then make sure they know what they are doing. The tribunal will work on the basis that your representative is familiar with the procedure and if they make a mistake (such as forgetting to get your claim in on time) the tribunal may be less sympathetic than if you were doing the job yourself. If you do not have anyone to represent you, the tribunal is likely to bend over backwards to be helpful and explain each stage of the process to you. You can ask your local tribunal for a free guide to tribunal procedure. The Equal Opportunities Commission has also produced a step-by-step guide which is free on request.

Making a Claim

Does your Employer Have an Internal Procedure?

Before you think about making a claim, you should usually exhaust your employer's internal grievance procedure. However, if that would mean missing the deadline for lodging your claim, then you must go ahead and start the process. It may be worth telling your employer in writing that you have done so, as starting a claim can sometimes induce a settlement. Unfortunately, it can also have the opposite effect. You should also be careful about time limits if your employer offers you alternative employment.

> In a recent case (*London Underground Ltd* v. *Noel*), the Court of Appeal said that a claim was time-barred, although the reason for the applicant's delay was that she had accepted the employer's offer of alternative employment. By the time the offer was withdrawn, she was outside the three-month time limit for bringing her claim.

If you want to be sure that you will not be time-barred, you should lodge your claim irrespective of what negotiations are going on.

If you do not make use of your employer's internal procedure (assuming you are aware that one exists), the tribunal can reduce the compensatory award (see below for details) by two weeks' pay. By the same token, if your employer does not allow you to use the internal appeal procedure (assuming there is one), the tribunal can award you extra compensation of two weeks' pay.

What Time Limits do you Need to Be Aware of?

Remember that you must bring your claim within the time limit set down by the law (see box below). So, if the discrimination took place on 12 July, then you need to have lodged the claim by 11 October. But remember that you cannot lodge your claim on a Saturday, Sunday or a bank holiday so if the deadline for your ET1 (the form you use for your applications) is 25 December, you have to make sure it arrives with the tribunal the day before.

If you are not going to deliver the form in person to the tribunal office, then you must allow at least two working days for delivery. It is, therefore, a good idea to send it recorded delivery. You may also fax your application to the office, but whatever method you use, remember to telephone the tribunal office to check whether it has arrived – sometimes even faxes can go astray.

Topic	Qualifying period	Time limit for bringing claim
Sex discrimination	None	Within three months (less one day) of act
Race discrimination	None	Within three months (less one day) of act
Disability discrimination	None	Within three months (less one day) of act
Equal pay	None	Within six months of termination of employment
Minimum wage	None	Within three months (less one day) of act
Working time regulations	None	Within three months (less one day) of act
Whistleblowing	None	Within three months of making the protected disclosure
Time off for public and union duties (paid and unpaid)	None	Within three months (less one day) of date of employer's failure
Unfair dismissal	One year	Within three months (less one day) of effective date of termination (see Chapter 6)

Topic	Qualifying period	Time limit for bringing claim
Redundancy payment	Two years	Within six months of effective date of termination
Written reasons for dismissal	One year	Within three months (less one day) of effective date of termination
Action short of dismissal	None	Within three months starting with date of last action complained of
Right to paid time off for ante-natal care	None	Within three months of date of appointment
Unlawful deduction from wages	None	Within three months from date of last deduction

How do you Know when Time Starts to Run?

Sometimes it can be difficult to know when the alleged act took place, making it difficult to know the date from when time should run. For instance, if there is a series of linked acts, the tribunal may say that time runs from the date of the last act. Alternatively, it may decide that each act has to be looked at separately.

> Take the case of *Cast* v. *Croydon College* which highlights the difficulty in assessing whether an act is the last in a series of breaches or one which stands on its own. In March 1992, when she was pregnant, Mrs Cast asked her employers if she could return on a job share or part-time basis. This was refused. After returning to work in early 1993, she again asked her employers on two occasions if she could work part time, but again she was refused. In June 1993, she resigned and claimed sex discrimination, but the original tribunal and employment appeal tribunal found against her, saying that there was no continuing act, just a repetition of the original request and refusal. She had therefore run out of time.

However, the Court of Appeal differed, finding that the employer's stance in refusing to allow her to work part time was a continuing act over a period of time within the meaning of the Sex Discrimination Act. It said that if a matter is considered again in response to a further request, then time begins to run again.

The effect of this decision is that if you make repeated requests to work, say, part time, the time limit runs from the date of the final refusal, as long as the employer thought about the matter again at that point. However, if your employer just rubberstamps the earlier decision, this will not be a fresh act of discrimination and time will run from the date when the request was last considered.

What is the Difference Between Continuous Discrimination and a Single Act?

It is very difficult to distinguish between continuous discrimination and a single act of discrimination which has a continuing effect. For example, a failed promotion attempt resulting in continued employment at a lower wage is not in itself continuing discrimination. In that instance, you would, therefore, have had to lodge a claim within three months of being told that you had not got the promotion. However, if the reason that you did not get the promotion was because of a policy by your employer to discriminate against women, members of ethnic minority groups, etc., that would be an example of continuing discrimination.

Note that a close sequence of discriminatory actions such as a series of threats, warnings or abuse in a case of harassment does not constitute continuing discrimination as far as the law is concerned. Your tribunal claim, therefore, needs to be lodged within three months of each incident. That applies even if the worker goes off sick and resigns – the time limit is not three months from the resignation, but three months from the last act of harassment.

If you have been dismissed and need to work out the effective date of termination, see Chapter 6 for details.

Can you Make a Claim Out of Time?

The tribunal will consider *discrimination* claims made out of time if it is 'just and equitable to do so'. However, the tribunal will want to know why you put the claim in late and you would have to give detailed reasons for the delay.

If your claim is one of *unfair dismissal*, then the test is much stricter. In these claims, the tribunal will only extend the time limit if it was not reasonably practicable for you to present the claim in time, perhaps because it was lost in the post (hence the importance of checking with the tribunal whether it has arrived) or because you were too ill to lodge it. If you engage a representative (which includes a trade union representative), the tribunal will assume that it was reasonably practicable for him or her to present the claim in time.

If the claim is for *equal pay*, the tribunal has no discretion for extending the six-month time limit.

What Complaint/s do you Want to Make?

Before you start your claim, you need to be clear about the basis of your complaint. In other words, make sure you know what you are complaining about – is it unfair dismissal, sex discrimination, redundancy pay, etc.?

You can bring more than one complaint and, if you want to do so, make sure that you include them all on the originating form – called an ET1 form – which you can obtain from any job centre, unemployment benefit office or the Equal Opportunities Commission. If you are not sure about whether to include something, it is better to incorporate it at this stage rather than have to apply to amend the ET1 at some later stage when you run the risk of being out of time.

Can you Ask Why you Have Been Dismissed?

If you have been dismissed, you should also ask your employer for written reasons for the dismissal within three months of the dismissal – your employer must comply within 14 days. If he or she fails to do so, you can claim compensation of two weeks' gross pay. Asking for written reasons can be a useful ploy because you can rely on them as evidence at the tribunal.

Will you Need Other Documentation?

It is also a good idea to collect any relevant documentation you may have before sending your form to the tribunal, as this may help you to write your supporting statement. This may include a statement of terms and conditions, pay slips, letter of dismissal, appraisal reports, equal opportunities policy, etc. If you do not have copies of any of these, ask your personnel department or your employer directly for them.

What Basic Information do you Need to Put on the Application Form?

To be valid, your application form must contain:

- Your name and address (you are known as the applicant)
- The name and address of the person you are claiming against (known as the respondent)
- The grounds on which you are bringing the complaint

If you are not sure of your employer's name and address, or you work for a number of associated companies and are not sure which one to put on the ET1, put them all in – that way, you will not miss anyone out.

What Other Information do you Need to Put on the Application Form?

If you are making more than one type of claim, make this clear on the form. For instance, state in the appropriate box the question/s that you want the tribunal to answer – whether you were unfairly dismissed or discriminated against on the ground of sex, race, etc.

If you are making a claim of indirect discrimination (see Chapter 3 for details), set the claim out in broad terms, giving alternative pools of employees with whom you are comparing yourself.

If you are claiming unfair dismissal, say on the form whether you want your employer to reinstate you in your old job, re-engage you in another job or pay you compensation. Other claims attract a remedy of compensation only.

Where do you Lodge the Application Form?

The ET1, also known as the originating application or notice of application, has to be lodged with the local tribunal of the employer's workplace. To find out which tribunal you should lodge your claim with, just telephone the Central Office Of Employment Tribunals (address at the end of the book). There is no charge for making an application.

Are you Allowed to Amend your ET1?

You can amend the ET1, but you will need either the agreement of the other side or the permission of the tribunal. Things get more complicated if your amendment drastically changes the basis of the claim, say from unfair dismissal to discrimination, not least because the other party is very likely not to agree to the change. In those circumstances, you will have to ask the tribunal for permission well in advance of the hearing.

In deciding whether to allow a substantial amendment, the tribunal will weigh up the potential injustice and inconvenience to the other side. For instance, allowing an amendment might delay proceedings and increase costs, but if these inconveniences can be justified then the tribunal is likely to agree to the amendment. However, if the amendment is being sought, say, because your adviser failed to fill in the form correctly then the tribunal may well refuse the request. The request may also be refused if you have run out of time. If, however, you just want to add a new respondent or amend the address, then it is very unlikely that such a request will be refused.

What Happens Once you Send in your Application Form?

Once the local tribunal office receives your ET1, it then sends a copy to the respondent – probably your employer. He or she then has to reply to your application within 21 days from the date of receipt by filling in what is known as an ET3 or a Notice of Appearance. Do not be surprised if your employer asks for more time to fill in the ET3 – this is very common – and the tribunal is very likely to agree to the request.

Your employer will not be allowed to defend your claim if he or she has not submitted an ET3 by the date of the hearing. But if he or she turns up at the hearing with it, it is up to the tribunal whether to accept it or not at such a late stage. It might order an adjournment and order the employer to pay your wasted costs for turning up that day.

What is the Questionnaire Procedure?

If you are claiming discrimination – whether on the basis of race, sex or disability – you are allowed to submit a questionnaire to the respondent asking just about anything you like (as long as it is somehow relevant to your claim). There are standard questionnaires which you can obtain from the Department of Education and Employment, your local job centre or the Equal Opportunities Commission, the Commission for Racial Equality and the Disability Rights Commission. It is probably better to use the form rather than draw up your own questionnaire.

When Should you Send the Questionnaire?

You can send your questionnaire *direct to your employer* any time within three months from the act of discrimination. It is a good idea to use recorded delivery, so that your employer cannot deny receipt of the questionnaire.

However, *once proceedings are issued* (that is, once your ET1 was received at the tribunal office), you need to send the questionnaire to your employer within 21 days of that date. Remember to allow time for delivery. For instance, if you send your complaint first class to the tribunal, allow for one day in the post and then add on 20 days to calculate your deadline.

It is all too easy to miss the 21-day deadline, and you should therefore send your questionnaire early in the proceedings to avoid any mishaps. However, if you do miss the deadline, you can ask the other side to agree to an extension or ask the tribunal for one. If, for whatever reason, the tribunal refuses, do not despair as you can always ask questions under Further and Better Particulars (see below).

Does your Employer Have to Reply to the Questionnaire?

The tribunal cannot force your employer to reply to the questions, but lots of employers do not realise this and it is worth encouraging this illusion by requesting a reply within 14 days of service. If your employer does not reply, be sure to tell the tribunal as it can draw an adverse inference from the failure to reply. In other words, it can interpret your employer's refusal as inference that there has been unlawful discrimination. If your employer does reply, you can submit the questionnaire as evidence to the tribunal. If your employer does not answer your questions properly, you can submit a second questionnaire, but you will need the tribunal's permission to do that.

What Questions Should you Ask?

The standard questionnaire form contains two printed questions, but you are entitled to ask additional questions. In fact, you can ask as many questions as you like, although if you ask too many, your employer may complain that the questionnaire is oppressive because of the amount of work involved in answering all the questions. However, if a lot of your questions are based on information that personnel can supply and are relevant to your case, then this argument is unlikely to wash with the tribunal.

Broadly speaking, you should ask two categories of questions:

- The first should be about the facts and circumstances of the particular treatment that you are complaining about
- The second should concentrate on eliciting statistical information, such as numbers of workers, numbers of ethnic minority workers, full-timers, etc. You can also ask questions about the workplace in general which might elicit information about how other workers have been treated in similar circumstances

Make sure that your questions are clear and reasonable – there is no point in giving your employer an excuse to avoid answering them. You should also make sure that your statement setting out the allegations is unambiguous so that your employer cannot argue that he or she does not understand what they are alleged to have done – an argument which frequently wins sympathy from a tribunal. And ensure that the grounds you set out in your ET1 for bringing the claim are the same as those you give in the questionnaire, otherwise you will be cross-examined on any differences.

What are Further and Better Particulars of the ET3?

If you do not understand anything that your employer has said in the ET3, you are entitled to ask for further information. You need to write to the other party, setting out the points which need clarification and asking specific questions with regard to each of those points. It is a good idea to ask for the information within 14 days of receipt of the letter, so that if none is forthcoming you can then go to the tribunal and ask them to order the employer to give you what you have asked for. If the employer also fails to respond to that order, you need to let the tribunal know because it has the power to stop the employer from continuing with his or her defence.

All that you can ask for is more details or 'particulars' of the employer's defence. For example, if the employer said in the ET3 that 'we investigated the applicant's claims and found no basis to them', a relevant request would be along the following lines: 'Please state the ways in which you investigated the applicant's claim, the people involved in the investigation and the date/s when it was carried out.' Whatever you do, don't try to use the exercise as a 'fishing' expedition – in other words, asking for information which is not related to anything the employer raised in the ET3.

What are Interrogatories?

This is an additional procedure allowing you to ask a series of questions, which, unlike further and better particulars, is not restricted to what the employer said in the ET3. Instead, this procedure allows you to ask questions about anything that the tribunal is going to have to make a decision about or to show that the information is likely to help the tribunal in dealing with the claim. Once again, if your employer fails to reply to your questions, you can write to the tribunal and ask for an order for the information.

How do you Get Hold of Documents that you Need?

The legal term for this is discovery, which just means the method by which you can obtain documents in the employer's possession. Again, you should ask the employer for the documentation in the first place, but if he or she refuses or fails to reply, then ask the tribunal to make an order.

Cases can be won or lost on the strength of the documentation before the tribunal and it is essential that you collate everything that is relevant and that you want to rely on before the hearing. Unfortunately, your employer is not obliged to tell you about all the relevant documentation in his or her possession, so you need to think about what the employer has and what you will need to prove your case.

The best thing to do is to ask your employer to list and disclose all documents relevant to the claim. If you know that there are certain documents which are of relevance, then ask for them specifically. Remember to give a deadline of 14 days by which the employer should reply. If he or she fails to do so, then you can legitimately go ahead and ask the tribunal to make an order.

When you do so, tell the tribunal that you have already asked the employer for discovery. It is also worth asking the tribunal to order what is known as 'full' discovery – in other words, all the relevant documents in your employer's possession, not just those on which he or she is going to rely.

Can you Bring Witnesses?

If you have anyone who can help your claim, then you should ask them to attend as a witness. However, current colleagues may be unwilling to appear on your behalf because to do so would blot their copy book with the employer. You can, however, apply to the tribunal for a witness order requiring that person to attend. In that way, your colleague can explain to your employer that he or she is not attending voluntarily. However, there is little point in getting an order for someone who really does not want to attend as they will invariably be a bad witness and will not help your case.

Any request needs to be sent to the tribunal in time for the hearing, giving the name and home or work address of the witness. You also need to say briefly why this person's evidence is relevant and explain that the witness will not attend voluntarily.

Will you Need Witness Statements?

The tribunal may ask for witness statements to be prepared. Therefore, you need, with the co-operation of your witness, to put together the detailed facts of what the witness will say at the hearing. Your witness can then rely on the statement at the hearing, where it is usually read out. Your representative can ask a few questions or the witness can add to it as he or she reads through it. You should also prepare a statement for yourself.

The tribunal may order you to exchange your witness statements with the other side some time before the hearing. This is to enable each side to read what the other will say at the hearing. The exchange must be simultaneous to stop one side or the other from changing what they were going to say in the light of the witness statement they received.

Do you Need an Agreed Bundle of Documents?

It is a good idea to prepare an agreed bundle of documents with the other side before the hearing – that way the tribunal only has to refer to one lot of papers and not two. Remember to prepare three copies for the tribunal panel members and enough for your witnesses, as well as one for each party. The bundle will contain:

- Your ET1
- Your employer's ET3
- Further and better particulars, interrogatories, tribunal orders, etc.
- Witness statements, although these can be handed in on the day unless there was an order for exchange
- Any other documents on which you or the other side will rely

You should prepare a contents page and paginate each page in the bundle so that everyone can find everything easily.

What is a Pre-trial Directions Hearing/Interlocutory Hearing?

This is an informal hearing before the chair of the tribunal sitting alone, attended only by the parties or their representatives. A directions hearing is not needed in every case, but it can be useful to deal with outstanding procedural issues that you have not been able to resolve with your employer, such as disclosure of documents, further and better particulars, etc. You can ask the tribunal to hold a directions hearing or the tribunal can decide to hold one.

What is a Preliminary Hearing?

This hearing can also be initiated by either side or ordered by the tribunal to decide whether your claim should be heard. For instance, the other side may ask for a hearing to ascertain whether you have enough qualifying service to bring an unfair dismissal claim, whether you are an employee, etc.

What is a Pre-hearing Review?

This hearing can also be asked for by either of the parties or ordered by the tribunal to decide whether your application has any chance of success. The tribunal will make the decision, solely on the basis of the representations made to it and the ET1 and ET3. If it decides that there are no reasonable prospects of success, it will require a deposit of £150 from you in order to proceed.

What Role does the Advisory, Conciliation and Arbitration Service (ACAS) Play?

Once you send in your ET1, your claim will automatically be forwarded to ACAS who will appoint a Conciliation Officer to see if a settlement can be reached with the other side. You do not have to reach a settlement, but it is useful if you can because it saves all the fuss and hassle of going to tribunal. It is also a useful way of negotiating a good reference as a term of the settlement.

The Conciliation Officer will not push you into a settlement, as he or she basically acts as honest broker between the two sides. All discussion is confidential with the ACAS officer – at least it should be.

What about Costs and Legal Aid?

If you win your claim, you are unlikely to be awarded any costs by the tribunal. This has an advantage for applicants because if you lose your claim, costs are just as unlikely to be awarded against you unless you withdraw at the last minute without any explanation or the tribunal thought that you were a complete time-waster.

Legal aid (that is, support from the state to bring a claim) is not available for tribunal cases. You may be eligible to receive free advice and assistance from a solicitor leading up to the case, but this is limited to a couple of hours and eligibility is means-tested.

At the Hearing

However trivial it may seem, it is important to look smart when you appear in front of the tribunal. A slovenly appearance may give the tribunal the impression that you will make a careless presentation. It is also very important to arrive on time, or better still with time to spare, not least because the other side might turn up with paperwork you haven't seen before and have to read before the hearing. If you are not there at the right time, the case is likely to be dismissed in your absence. If you are going to be late, you must ring the tribunal and explain.

Will there Be Publicity?

Tribunal hearings are usually open to the public, including the press. However, in certain circumstances – such as in cases of sexual harassment – you can ask the tribunal to make a restricted reporting order which means that the media cannot publish the names of either the applicant or the respondent during the tribunal hearing. Once the hearing comes to an end, the media are then free to publish all details of the hearing.

What is the Order of Events?

- Usually the applicant kicks off, except in unfair dismissal claims when the employer starts proceedings. (But note that if the employer is disputing whether there was a dismissal you go first.) Always call the chair 'sir' or 'madam'
- Whoever starts can make an opening statement, although some tribunals dispense with this step now

- Assuming that you go first as the applicant, you will give evidence and can then be cross-examined by the other side. This just means that you can be asked questions about anything you have said. If you are represented, you may be asked further questions about anything that came up in cross-examination. Otherwise, you can make a statement to clarify anything that came up in cross-examination
- The tribunal panel can then ask questions
- You can then call your witnesses who may read from their statements. You can ask supplementary questions. The respondent will then cross-examine each of them and the tribunal may ask questions. You can then re-examine your witnesses
- It is then the respondent's turn to go through the same process
- Each party sums up
- The tribunal's decision is usually unanimous, although it can be by majority. It may not make its decision immediately – sometimes it will take weeks – and will be sent to the parties by post
- In cases of discrimination or trade union activities, the tribunal must give full written reasons for its decision. Otherwise it can choose whether to give full or summary reasons

What is the Standard of Proof?

Once the tribunal has heard all the evidence, it has to determine the case on the 'balance of probabilities'. This means that the tribunal has to decide that it was 'more probable than not' that you were discriminated against or dismissed for whatever reason. This is a much lower standard of proof than the criminal courts, where a charge has to be proved 'beyond reasonable doubt'.

Can you Appeal Against the Decision of a Tribunal?

You have a right to appeal, on a point of law, to the Employment Appeal Tribunal, within 42 days of the date that the tribunal's decision is sent to you.

If you feel your claim was prejudiced by the conduct of the tribunal panel – perhaps with interruptions or a refusal to let you call evidence – you can use such behaviour as a ground of appeal against the decision, as long as you object at the time and ask the tribunal to note your objection.

Remedies and Compensation

Before you start proceedings, you need to know what you want to achieve. If you are claiming unfair dismissal, you have to decide on the ET1 form whether you want your old job back, whether you would accept a different job with your old employer or whether you just want compensation. There is no point, for instance, in bringing an unfair dismissal claim if all you want is a reference. If you are bringing a discrimination claim, then the only remedy available is compensation.

Should you Settle the Claim with the Help of ACAS?

As explained above, most claims are referred to ACAS, which has a statutory duty to promote a settlement, although their officers cannot force you to settle. Any agreement reached through ACAS is binding on both parties, so that neither of you can go back and change the terms. If you manage to reach a settlement with the employer directly, you still have to tell the ACAS officer if they have been involved.

What is a Compromise Agreement?

The only other way to reach an enforceable settlement is to use a lawyer or some other independent adviser. If you do so, the agreement (known as a compromise agreement) must satisfy the following terms:

* Be in writing
* State that you have received independent advice from an adviser who is covered by professional indemnity insurance
* State that you have received independent legal advice explaining the terms of the agreement and that you cannot pursue the claim in an employment tribunal or any other court
* Relate to the particular complaint that you wanted to bring to a tribunal

Ideally, only the particular tribunal claim should be settled, but in practice most employers insist on a wider settlement. In other words, in return for an agreed sum, you waive your right to all other claims arising out of the contract of employment. It is advisable to include a date by which the payment is to be made, giving you time to submit your tribunal claim if the employer fails to cough up.

If you want a reference from your employer, this can be negotiated as part of the compromise agreement. If your employer refuses and you can show that this was because you brought (or threatened to bring) proceedings, this amounts to victimisation and you can bring a claim against the employer on that basis (see Chapter 1 for details of what happened in *Coote* v. *Granada Hospitality Ltd*).

What Compensation are you Entitled to for Unfair Dismissal?

If the tribunal does not order re-instatement or re-engagement or you have only claimed compensation, you will receive an award made up of two components:

- The basic award, which is calculated on the basis of the number of years of continuous employment with that employer, up to a maximum of 20, as follows:

  1. Up to age 21 – half a week's pay per year of service
  2. From age 22 to 40 – one week's pay per year of service
  3. From age 41 to 65 – one and a half week's pay per year of service

  The weekly pay is limited to a set amount – currently £230 – which is updated once a year. So, for instance, if you worked for 15 years between the ages of 22 to 40, and were earning £300 per week, you can expect the grand total of 15 x £230 which equals £3,450

- The compensatory award which compensates you for the loss you have suffered, currently limited to £50,000. Under this heading you can claim for:

  1. Loss of earnings between the date of the dismissal and the date of the tribunal hearing
  2. Loss of future earnings (which will be affected by your age, the state of the labour market, the likelihood that you would have remained in that job, etc. This calculation is, by definition, an inexact science)

3. Loss of benefits such as pension rights, health insurance, maternity benefits
4. Reasonable expenses incurred in trying to find other work
5. Interest, if not paid within 42 days of the tribunal's order

The total award will be an amount which the tribunal considers just and equitable in the circumstances, but it will be reduced if the tribunal thinks that you were partly to blame for the dismissal or that you did not mitigate your loss (see below). Tribunals can also reduce the award if you did not make use of the employer's internal appeals procedure.

If your employer fails to comply with an order of the tribunal to re-engage or re-instate you, it will make an additional award to you which is between 13 and 26 weeks' pay.

Can you Claim your Pay for the Notice Period?

If your employer dismisses you without notice and does not give you any pay in lieu, you are entitled to include a claim for net pay for the statutory or contractual notice period (whichever is the longer) in your claim for immediate loss if there is a payment in lieu clause in your contract. This applies even if you find other work during the notice period.

> For instance, in a recent case (*Cerberus Software Ltd* v. *Rowley*), the contract stated that either party could terminate on giving six months' notice. It also said that the employers could make a payment in lieu of notice. Mr Rowley was dismissed without notice on 26 June 1997, but was not given any money in lieu. He obtained new employment on 1 August, but the Employment Appeal Tribunal said that he was entitled to receive the full amount as that was what was due under the contract.

If you waive your right to the statutory notice period, you cannot then make a claim for a payment in lieu because there is no breach in that situation.

What Compensation are you Entitled to for Redundancy?

See Chapter 6.

What Compensation are you Entitled to for Discrimination?

Unlike unfair dismissal, there is no limit on the amount of the award in sex, race or disability claims, whether direct or indirect. Average awards of compensation in sex discrimination cases hover around £7,000 and about £6,000 in race cases, whereas in disability claims they are about £10,000.

You can make a claim for the following:

- Loss of earnings from the date of the act of discrimination to the date of the tribunal hearing, less any earnings in a new job over that period
- Loss of future earnings, which involves working out how long it may take you to find another job on the basis of availability of work and how much you are likely to get paid. If you were dismissed because you wanted to work part time, you have to restrict your claim to the number of hours you asked to work
- Loss of opportunity, for instance, if you were not shortlisted for interview for a job. The tribunal will have to consider how long you might have stayed in the job and how long it will take you to find other work
- Loss of benefits such as pension, company car, health insurance
- Expenses incurred in looking for other work
- Injury to feelings
- Personal injury, which can include psychiatric damage such as a claim for post-traumatic stress disorder
- Aggravated damages if the employer has behaved in a high-handed way towards you which has aggravated the injury to your feelings, such as refusing to apologise or not investigating the grievance seriously
- Interest payable on the award for injury to feelings

If your employer fails to comply with the tribunal's order, it can make an additional award of between 26 and 52 weeks' pay.

What Compensation are you Entitled to for a Reason Related to Pregnancy?

If your claim is for pregnancy discrimination, the tribunal will consider the following:

- The percentage chance that you would have returned to work. If it is clear that you had every intention of returning, then the tribunal will not reduce your claim for loss of earnings
- Your efforts to mitigate your loss from six months after the birth of your child

What Compensation are you Entitled to in an Equal Pay Claim?

You will be entitled to one of two things:

- An award of arrears of pay for up to six years
- Damages for breach of a term of the contract which is not to do with pay

What are the Consequences if you Fail to Mitigate your Loss?

If you resign or are dismissed, you must look for another job in order to mitigate your loss. This simply means that the tribunal will expect you to try and find other work so that your claim for loss of earnings will be reduced as much as possible. If you fail to do so, the tribunal may reduce your claim for compensation. You should therefore keep copies of all job applications you have made and any rejection letters received. It is also a good idea to keep evidence of how much it has cost you to look for work, such as stamps, travel, etc.

It is worth noting that it is for your employer to prove a failure to mitigate. If he or she cannot produce any evidence that you have not mitigated your loss (what you should have done and when), the tribunal cannot make an assumption about when you might have found other work, had you mitigated your loss. Nevertheless, it is much better if you bring evidence with you to the tribunal of all efforts you have made to find new work.

If you find work soon after your dismissal or resignation which is paid as well or better than your previous employment and has equivalent benefits, the tribunal will not make you an award for loss of earnings, loss of future earnings or loss of benefits. You can still make a claim for injury to feeling and, if appropriate, aggravated damages.

8
General

Useful Addresses

Advisory, Conciliation and Arbitration Service (ACAS)
Head Office:
Brandon House
180 Borough High Street
London SE1 1LW

ACAS Public Enquiry points

Birmingham	0121 456 5856
Bristol	0117 974 4066
Cardiff	029 20761126
Fleet	01252 811868
Glasgow	0141 204 2677
Leeds	0113 243 1371
Liverpool	0151 427 8881
London	020 7396 5100
Manchester	0161 228 3222
Newcastle-upon-Tyne	0191 261 2191
Nottingham	0115 969 3355

Employment Tribunals general enquiry line 0345 959775

Commission for Racial Equality
Elliot House
10–12 Allington Street
London SW1E 5EH
Tel: 020 7828 7022

Disability Rights Commission
2nd floor, Arndale House
The Arndale Centre
Manchester M4 3AQ
Tel: 0161 261 1700

Equal Opportunities Commission
Overseas House
Quay Street
Manchester M3 3HN
Tel: 0161 833 9244

Health and Safety Executive contact points:

Basingstoke	01256 404 000
Birmingham	0121 607 6200
Bristol	01179 886 000
Cardiff	029 2026 3000
Chelmsford	01245 706 200
East Grinstead	01342 334 200
Edinburgh	0131 247 2000
Glasgow	0141 275 3000
Leeds	0113 283 4200
London	020 7556 2100
Luton	01582 444 200
Manchester	0161 952 8200
Merseyside	0151 479 2200
Newcastle-under-Lyme	01782 602 300
Newcastle-upon-Tyne	0191 202 6200
Northampton	01604 738 300
Nottingham	01159 712 800
Preston	01772 836 200
Sheffield	0114 291 2300

Incomes Data Services
77 Bastwick Street
London EC1V 3TT
Tel: 020 7250 3434

Industrial Relations Services
Eclipse Group Ltd
18–20 Highbury Place
London N5 1QP
Tel: 020 7354 5858

Maternity Alliance
45 Beech Street
London EC2P 2LX
Tel: Advice Line 020 7588 8582
      Office 020 7588 8583

New Ways to Work
309 Upper Street
London N1 2TY
Tel: 020 7930 3355

Rights of Women
52–54 Featherstone Street
London EC1V 8RT
Tel: 020 7251 6575

Trades Union Congress
Congress House
Great Russell Street
London WC1B 3LS
Tel: 020 7636 4030

References

Commission for Racial Equality, *Enforcing the Race Relations Act, A Code of Practice for the CRE*, 1995

Doyle, Brian, *Disability Discrimination, Law and Practice*, Jordan Publishing Ltd, 1996

Equal Opportunities Commission, *Towards Equality, A Casebook of Decisions on Sex Discrimination and Equal Pay*, 1995 and 1997

—— *The Sex Discrimination Act and Advertising*, undated

Ford, Michael, *Surveillance and Privacy at Work*, Institute of Employment Rights, 1998

Fredman, Sandra, *Women and the Law*, Clarendon Press, 1997

Incomes Data Services, *Disability Discrimination Act 1995*, Employment Law Supplement 78, October 1996

—— *Sex Discrimination and Equal Pay*, Employment Law Handbook, December 1998

—— *Race discrimination*, Employment Law Handbook, 1999

—— *Unfair Dismissal*, Employment Law Handbook, August 1998

—— *Employment Rights Act 1996*, Employment Law Supplement 77, August 1996

—— *Contracts of Employment*, Employment Law Handbook, April 1998

—— *IT Practice and Procedure*, Employment Law Handbook, July 1994

—— *Employees and the Criminal Law*, Employment Law Supplement 74, August 1995

Morris, Anne and O'Donnell, Therese (eds), *Feminist Perspectives on Employment Law*, Cavendish Publishing Ltd, 1999

Palmer, Camilla, *Legal Rights to Child-Friendly Working Hours*, Maternity Alliance, 1998

Table of Cases

Abdoulaye & ors *v.* Régie Nationale des Usines Renault SA (ECJ 16.9.99 (C-218/09), 53

Adams *v.* Strathclyde Regional Council (EAT no 456/88), 14

Adekeye *v.* The Post Office (No 2) (1997, IRLR 105), 71

Allonby *v.* Accrington and Rossendale College and ors (EAt 1300/97 and 1080/98), 41

Arbeiterwholfahrt der Stadt Berlin *v.* Botel (1992 IRLR 423), 59, 111

Barber and others *v.* RJB Mining (UK) Ltd (1999, IRLR 308), 147
Barratt Developments (Bradford) Ltd *v.* UCATT (1977, IRLR 403), 183
Barry *v.* Midland Bank (1999, IRLR 581), 180
Bartholomew *v.* London Borough of Hackney (1999, IRLR 246), 21
Bilka-Kaufhaus GmbH *v.* Weber von Hartz (1986, IRLR 317), 69
Boychuk *v.* HJ Symons Holdings Ltd (1977, IRLR 395), 120
British Sugar *v.* Kirker (1998, IRLR 624), 187
Burton *v.* De Vere Hotels (1996, IRLR 596), 64
Carmichael *v.* National Power plc (2000, IRLR 43), 33
Caruana *v.* Manchester Airport plc (1996, IRLR 378), 33
Cast *v.* Croydon College (1998, IRLR 318), 60, 199
Caulker *v.* Bluebird Foodmarket and ors (ET no 2204522/97), 38
Cerberus Software Ltd *v.* Rowley (EAT 4.5.99. Case No 1023/98), 213
Clark *v.* TDG Ltd t/a Novacold (1999, IRLR 318), 77
Clarke *v.* Ely (IMI) Kynoch Ltd (1982 IRLR 482), 59
Clymo *v.* London Borough of Wandsworth (1989, IRLR 241), 88
Coker and Osamor *v.* Lord Chancellor and Lord Chancellor's Department (1999, IRLR 396), 5
Colclough *v.* Staffordshire County Council (unreported, 1994), 142
Coote *v.* Granada Hospitality Ltd (1999, IRLR 452), 22, 71, 212
Coyne *v.* The Home Office (23.4.99 EAT 244/97), 163
Davies *v.* Neath Port Talbot County Borough Council (1999, IRLR 769), 59, 112
Day *v.* T Pickles Farms Ltd (1999, IRLR 217), 55
Dekker *v.* Stichting Vormingscentrum voor Jonge Volwassen (VJV Centrum) Plus (1991, IRLR 27), 19
Delaney *v.* Staples (1991, ICR 331), 96, 97
Dhanjal *v.* British Steel General Steels (ET Case No 50740/91), 121
Diocese of Hallam Trustee *v.* Connaughton (1996, IRLR 505), 41
East Lindsay District Council *v.* Daubney (1977, IRLR 181), 129
Enderby and ors *v.* Frenchay Health Authority and ors (1992, IRLR 15), 47
Finn *v.* South Wales Constabulary (Central Office of Industrial Tribunals 3102/62), 117
Garbett & ors *v.* Sierotko (2.12.98 ET Case Nos 2406815/97; 2406820/97; 2400083/98), 123
Gates *v.* Security Express Guards (ET Case No 45142/92), 162
Hairsine *v.* Kingston upon Hull City Council (1992, ICR 212), 111
Hale and Clunie *v.* Wiltshire Healthcare NHS Trust (ET/1401250/98;

1401251/98), 66

Halford v. United Kingdom (1997, IRLR 471), 123

Halfpenny v. IGE Medical Systems (1999, IRLR 177), 129

Hanlon v. University of Huddersfield (EAT, 1998), 79

Harvest Press Ltd v. McCaffrey (1999, IRLR 778), 161

Hayes v. Attorney-General (settled out of court), 6

Healy v. William B Morrison & Son Ltd (30.6.99. EAT number 172/99), 188

High Table Ltd v. Horst & ors (1997 IRLR 513) (see under Horst)

Hill v. General Accident Fire and Life Assurance Corporation plc (1998, IRLR 641), 129

Hitchcock v. Post Office (1980, ICR 100), 32

H J Heinz Co Ltd v. Kenrick (2000, IRLR 144), 79

Home Office v. Holmes (1984 IRLR 299), 59

Horst and ors v. High Table Ltd (1997, IRLR 513), 115, 179

Hurley v. Mustoe (1981, IRLR 208), 12

Hussain v. Alfred Brown (Worsted Mills) Ltd (ET no 1805479/98), 18

Insitu Cleaning Co Ltd & anor v. Heads (1995, IRLR 4), 162

Isa and Rashid v. BL Cars Ltd (ET Nos 27083/80 and 32273/79), 10

Janciuk v. Winerite Ltd (1998, IRLR 63), 176

Jenkins v. Kingsgate Clothing Productions (1981 IRLR 228), 59

Jepson and Dyas-Elliott v. The Labour Party and ors (1996, IRLR 116), 19

Johnstone v. Bloomsbury Health Authority (1991, IRLR 118), 28, 167

Jones v. Tower Boot Co Ltd (1997, IRLR 168), 63

Kapfunde v. Abbey National plc (1998, IRLR 584), 25

Kenny v. Hampshire Constabulary (1999, IRLR 76), 79

Kuratorium für Dialyse und Nierentransplantation v. Lewark (1996, IRLR 637), 59, 111

LA Goold (Pearmak) Ltd v. McConnell and anor (1995, IRLR 516), 28

Lancaster v. Birmingham City Council (5.7.99. Case No BM6 24958), 167

Lawrence and ors v. Regent Office Care Ltd and ors (1999, IRLR 148), 41

Levez v. TH Jennings (Harlow Pools) (1999, IRLR 764), 42

Lewen v. Denda (2000, IRLR 67), 48

London Borough of Croydon v. Kuttappan (18.1.99, EAT no 1292/98), 9

London Underground Ltd v. Noel (1999, IRLR 621), 197

London Underground *v.* Edwards (No 2) (1998, IRLR 364), 68
Macarthys Ltd *v.* Smith (1980, IRLR 210), 41
McCausland *v.* Dungannon District Council (1993, IRLR 583), 67
McGuigan *v.* T G Baynes & Sons (24.11.98. EAT number 1114/97), 188
Meade-Hill and National Union of Civil and Public Servants *v.* British
    Council (1995, IRLR 478), 114
Mrs J Woodhead *v.* Chief Constable of West Yorkshire police (EAT no
    285/89), 14
Murray & anor *v.* Foyle Meats Ltd (1999, IRLR 562), 179
Nagarajan *v.* London Regional Transport (1999, IRLR 572), 71
Narich Proprietary Ltd *v.* Commissioner of Pay-Roll Tax (1984, ICR
    286), 32
Nash *v.* Mash/Roe Group Ltd (1998, IRLR 168), 84
New Century Cleaning Co. Ltd *v.* Church (2000, IRLR 27), 96
O'Kelly *v.* Trusthouse Forte (1983, ICR 728), 32
O'Neill *v.* Symm & Co Ltd (1998, IRLR 233), 76
Pickstone *v.* Freemans plc (1988, IRLR 357), 45
Polkey *v.* AE Dayton Services Limited (1987, IRLR 503), 129, 172, 183
Price *v.* Civil Service Commission and anor (1978, IRLR 3), 84
R *v.* Attorney General for Northern Ireland ex parte Burns (1999,
    IRLR 315), 151
R *v.* Secretary of State for Employment ex parte EOC (1994, IRLR
    176), 59
Rainey *v.* Greater Glasgow Health Board (1987, IRLR 26), 46
Reed and anor *v.* Stedman (1999, IRLR 299), 163
Rideout *v.* TC Group (1998, IRLR 628), 17, 78
Rinner-Kuhn *v.* FWW Spezial-Gebaudereiningung GmbH & Co (1989
    IRLR 493), 59
Sagar *v.* H Ridehalgh & Son Ltd (1931, 1 CH 310), 29
Sanderson *v.* BAA plc (19.6.98, Case no 3202717/97), 68
Sarker *v.* South Tees Acute Hospitals NHS Trust (1997, IRLR 329), 24
Saunders *v.* Richmond-upon-Thames (1977, IRLR 362), 16
Schmidt *v.* Austicks Bookshops Ltd (1977, IRLR 360), 120
Scott *v.* Norfolk House Hotel (ET no 19715/82), 18
Scullard *v.* Knowles (1996, IRLR 344), 41
Secretary of State for Scotland *v.* Taylor (1999, IRLR 362), 30
Sidhu *v.* Aerospace Composite Technology Ltd (2000, IRLR 602), 62
SIMAP *v.* Conselleria de Sanidad y Consumo de la Generalidad
    Valenciana (ECJ, 3.10.00, C-303/98)

Smith and Grady *v.* United Kingdom (1999, IRLR 734), 82
Smith *v.* Safeway plc (1995, 132), 120
Springboard Sunderland Trust *v.* Robson (1992, IRLR 261), 44
Sreekanta *v.* Medical Relief Agency (Stoke on Trent) Ltd (EAT 536/91), 32
Stark *v.* Post Office (2000, ICR 1013), 143
Strathclyde Regional Council *v.* Porcelli (1986, IRLR 134), 161
Taylor *v.* Secretary of State for Scotland (2000, IRLR 502), 30, 84
Wakeman and ors *v.* Quick Corporation and anor (1999, IRLR 424), 63
Walker *v.* Northumberland County Council (1995, 1 All ER 737), 166
Waltons and Morse *v.* Dorrington (1997, IRLR 488), 28
Weathersfield Ltd t/a Van & Truck Rentals *v.* Sargent (1999, IRLR 94), 63
Western Excavating *v.* Sharp (1978, ICR 221), 174
Zafar *v.* Glasgow City Council (1998, IRLR 36), 72

Table of Statutes

Access to Medical Reports Act 1988, 127
Asylum and Immigration Act 1996, 36–8
Data Protection Act 1998, 130–4
Disability Discrimination Act 1995, 6, 8, 10, 11, 13, 16–17, 18, 20, 25, 33, 57, 72–82, 88, 127, 128, 153, 165, 168, 194, 195
Employment Relations Act 1999 (see under Employment Rights Act 1996)
Employment Rights Act 1996, 27, 30, 33, 48–52, 94–8, 105, 127, 161, 170, 180, 194–5
Equal Pay Act 1970, 2, 30, 33, 40, 41–7, 59–60, 88, 194
Equal Pay Directive 1975, 40, 57
Equal Treatment Directive 1976, 57, 86
Factory and Workshop Act 1891, 39
Fixed Term Workers Directive, 34–5
Health and Safety at Work Act 1974, 30, 137–8, 157–8, 159, 160, 168
Human Rights Act 1998, 82, 117, 122, 123–4, 134–5, 163, 166
National Minimum Wage Act 1998, 32, 35, 98–105
Parental Leave Directive, 89–90
Pensions Act 1995, 40
Protection from Harassment Act 1997, 160

Public Interest Disclosure Act 1998, 192–5

Race Relations Act 1976, 6, 7–8, 18, 19–20, 33, 36, 37, 61–72, 76, 77, 81, 85–8, 121, 161–2, 165, 168, 194, 195

Rehabilitation of Offenders Act 1974, 22–3

Sex Discrimination Act 1975, 2, 6, 7–8, 18, 19–20, 22, 30, 33, 40, 49, 57, 58, 59–60, 61–72, 76, 77, 81, 82, 85–8, 120–1, 161–2, 165, 168, 194, 195, 199–200

Trade Union and Labour Relations (Consolidation) Act 1992, 30, 108–12

Transport and Works Act 1992, 125

Table of Regulations

Control of Substances Hazardous to Health (COSHH) Regulations 1994, 145

Health and Safety (Display Screen Equipment) Regulations 1992, 144–5

Management of Health and Safety At Work (Amendment) Regulations 1994, 55, 140, 142

Management of Health and Safety At Work Regulations 1992, 54, 138–40, 150, 158, 159, 160, 168

Manual Handling Operations Regulations 1992, 140–2, 159

Part-Time Workers (Prevention of Less Favourable Treatment) Regulations 2000, 57–9, 60, 89

Personal Protective Equipment At Work Regulations 1992, 142–3, 159

Provision and Use of Work Equipment Regulations 1992, 143

Safety Critical Work Regulations 1994, 124

Sex Discrimination (Gender Reassignment) Regs 1999

Transfer of Undertakings (Protection of Employment) Regulations 1981, 30, 178

Working Time Regulations 1998, 52, 146–57

Workplace (Health, Safety and Welfare) Regulations 1992, 56, 143–4, 159

Index

ACAS (Advisory, Conciliation and Arbitration Service) 208, 211
Accident Legal Advice Service 159
'adverse inference' 18, 72
advertisements
    and discrimination 5–8
    exceptions 6, 7–8
age discrimination 83–5
    and job descriptions 10, 83
    making a claim 84–5
    and redundancy selection 83, 84, 186, 187
alcoholism 74
amputation 74
annual leave 154–6
    carrying over 155
    entitlement 154
    giving notice 155–6
    pay 155
ante-natal care, time-off for 54
appeals 172
applications see claims; job applications
appraisals 86
apprentices, and equal pay 42
aptitude tests 13
asthma 74

benefits, facilities and services, access to 87–8
blindness 73

bonus payments
    and discrimination 48
    and maternity leave 53
    see also wages
Braille 11, 73
Breach of Contract
    claiming damages 23–4
    and probationary period 36
    and wage deductions 97
    and wrongful dismissal 175–6
    see also contract of employment
breastfeeding, in workplace 56
bulimia nervosa 74

casual workers, and employment status 32–3
cerebral palsy 73
claims
    appeals against decision 210
    application form (ET1) 201, 202–3
        amendment of 202–3
        delivering 198
    compromise agreement 211–12
    costs and legal aid 209
    documentation 201, 206
        agreed bundle of 207–8
    employer's reply to (ET3) 203
    failure to mitigate loss 215
    hearings 209–10
        pre-trial hearings 208

claims *continued*
    and publicity 209
    information from employer
        203–6
    and internal procedure 197
    more than one 201, 202
    and representation 196–7
    standard of proof 210
    time limits 60, 197–201, 204
        extension of 200–1
    and time of alleged act
        199–200
    and witnesses 206–7
    see also Notice of Appearance
        (ET3)
clothing/appearance
    at hearing 209
    at work 118–21
    health and safety regulations
        119, 121
colitis 74
commission workers 102–3
compensation
    equal pay claims 215
    and internal appeal procedure
        197
    pregnancy discrimination
        214–15
    redundancy 180, 187
    unfair dismissal 202, 211,
        212–13
constructive dismissal 171, 173–5
    bringing a claim 175
    and change of contract 93
    proving 174
    and refusal to be searched 122
    and resignation 174–5
    see also dismissal; unfair dis-
        missal
contract of employment 26–30
    changing terms of 27, 92–4
    express terms of 27
    fixed-term 33–5
    implied terms of 27–9
    and incorporation of terms
        29–30
    and job mobility 114, 115

for job sharers 61
    and notice period 94
    and probationary period 35–6
    terms imposed by legislation 30
    written 27
    Zero Hours 35
contract workers, and equal pay 42
convictions
    disclosing 22–3
    and offer of employment 23

data protection *see* personal data
dependants
    definition of 91
    time-off for 90–1
depression 74
diabetes 74
disability
    assessing 74–6
    conditions excluded 74
    and confidentiality 16
    definition of 73–4
    and employers' awareness of
        79–80
    long-term 75
    and mental illness 74
    and normal day-to-day activities
        75–6
    and part-time work 57
    and positive discrimination 20
    'reasonable adjustments' 16–17,
        78–9, 80
disability discrimination 72–82
    and advertisements 6
    and application forms 11
    and aptitude tests 13
    and benefits 88
    bringing a claim 73
    comparators 77–8
    definition of 76–7
    employers' justification for 78,
        80–1
    and employment agencies 8
    and employment offers 18
    and interviews 16–17
    and job descriptions 10
    and medical testing 24, 25

and promotion, training and
transfer 88
and providing service for
disabled 72–3
and redundancy 187
and stress 168
and victimisation 81
disciplinary procedure, failure to
follow 176
'discovery' 12, 13, 21, 67, 206
discrimination
by employees 63–4, 82
comparators 62
compensation 214–15
continuous *v.* single act of 200
direct 61–2
and employers' responsibility
63–5, 82
indirect 46, 65–70, 114, 117,
187, 202
proving 62–3, 72
discrimination questionnaire 12,
18, 21, 42, 67, 203–5
employer's reply 204
types of questions 204–5
dismissal 169–95
definition of 169
effective date of termination
(EDT) 191
of employees having relationship 117–18
fair reasons for 170–1
and giving notice 175–6
and gross misconduct 118,
176–7, 181, 189
on health grounds 125, 126,
127, 128–30
and health and safety regulations 119
of husband and wife teams 118
procedural fairness 172
reasonableness of 171–2
right of appeal 172–3
for whistleblowing 194
written reasons 171, 201
see also constructive dismissal;
notice period; redundancy;

summary dismissal; unfair
dismissal; wrongful dismissal
domestic incidents, and time-off
90–1
dress codes 120–1
see also clothing/appearance;
uniform
drug tests
employers' rights 124–5
and health and safety 125
dysmenorrhoea 126

educational qualifications 10–11
overseas 12
effective date of termination (EDT)
191
emphysema 74
employees
discrimination by 63–4, 82
obligations 29, 138, 139
rights 121–2, 134–5
employers
defence against discrimination
claims 64–5
and defence of pay difference
46–7
duty of care 136–7, 167
employing women from overseas
36–8
information from 203–6
see also discrimination questionnaire
obligations of 28, 137–8, 140–5,
157–8, 159–61, 166–7
reviewing pay system 40–1
employment agencies 8
employment offers
Breach of Contract 23–4
conditional offers 24
and discrimination 17–19
and reasons for refusing candidate 18–19, 107–8
selection criteria 9, 11–13
terms of 17–18
employment status 30–6
casual workers 32–3
determining 31–2

employment status *continued*
  and employment rights 26
  homeworkers 33–4
  and mutuality of obligation 32,
    33
  women from overseas 36–8
epilepsy 74
Equal Opportunities Commission,
    Code of Practice 40–1
equal pay 39, 40–7
  backdating a claim 42
  benefits covered 42
  bringing a claim 41–7
  employers' defence 46–7
  comparators 41–2
  compensation 215
  'equal value' 44–6
  and indirect discrimination 46–7
  job evaluation study (JES) 43–4
  legislation 40–1
  'like work' 42–3, 45
  'work rated as equivalent' 43, 45
  see also pay systems; wages
establishment, definition 182–3
evidence
  'but for' test 62–3
  'discovery' 12, 13, 21, 67, 206
  employers' records 104–5
  and 'inference' 18, 72
  medical 126
  witnesses 206–7
exhibitionism 74
eye tests 145

fertility treatment, time off for 54
fixed-term contract
  and discrimination 34
  and employment rights 33–5
  number of renewals 35
'further and better particulars' 206

gagging clauses 194
gays and lesbians 82–3
genuine occupational qualification
    (GOQ) 7
gross misconduct
  during notice period 181, 189

investigation 176–7
and relationships at work 118
gross salary, calculation of 99–100

harassment 159–66
  based on disability 162, 165
  bringing a claim 164
  criminal offence 160
  employers' obligations 159–61,
    163–4
  failure to investigate 163–4
  and health 160
  and human rights 166
  introducing policy on 165
  and psychological injury 159
  racial 161, 162
  same sex discrimination 162
  sexual 161–2
  single act of 162
  steps to take 164–5
  and unfair dismissal 161, 163
  as unwelcome conduct 162–3
hay fever 74
health and safety at work 136–68
  and common law 136–7, 159–60
  and display screen equipment
    144–5
  employees obligations 138, 139
  employers' obligations 137–8,
    140–5, 157–8, 159–61, 166–7
  and equipment 143
  and hazardous substances 145
  health survey 139
  manual handling 140–2
  and pregnant workers 140, 142
  protective clothing 142–3
  risk assessment 54–6, 138–40,
    141, 145, 158
  stress 166–8
  training and information 137,
    142, 143, 145, 157
  and working alone 158–9
  and working time 146–56
  and workplace 143–4
  see also harassment; violence
hearing loss 73
holiday pay 155

homeworkers
    and defective equipment 159
    and employment status 32–3
    and equal pay 42
    and health and safety 158–9
    and minimum wage 102–4
human rights legislation, and
        employment 134–5
husband and wife employees 118

indirect discrimination 65–70
    criteria for 65–6
    and equal pay 46–7
    getting information 67
    and redundancy 187
    and relationships at work 117
    see also requirements or condi-
        tions
'inference' 18, 72
interim relief 106
interlocutory hearing 208
interrogatories 206
interviews 9, 13–17
    adjustments for disabled 16–17,
        78
    and disability discrimination 16
    and medical questions 15–16
    questions about domestic life 13,
        14–15

job applications
    forms 9, 10–11
    rejection of 8, 9, 18–19
job descriptions/specifications 9–10
job evaluation study (JES) 43–4
    analytical 44
job mobility 114–16
    and contract of employment
        114, 115
    and reasonable notice 115
    and redundancy 115–16
job sharing 61

last in, first out (LIFO) 185
legal aid 209
lifting/carrying 140–2
'like work' 42–3, 45

manual handling 140–2
marital status 10, 13, 14
'material factor defence' 45–6
Maternity Allowance 53–4
Maternity Certificate 49, 53
maternity leave
    additional leave 50–1
    entitlement 49
    failure to give notification 52
    giving notice to employer 49–51,
        52, 53
    and holidays 52
    and occupational pension 54
    and performance-related
        payments 48
    'qualifying week' 53
    and redundancy 187
    returning part-time 57
    returning to work 50, 51–2, 116
    and selection for redundancy
        56–7
    and service-related benefits 47
    and sick leave 50, 51, 52
    start of 50
    and Statutory Maternity Pay
        52–4
    and unfair dismissal 116, 188
    see also pregnancy-related
        sickness
maternity pay see Maternity
        Allowance; Statutory
        Maternity Pay
maternity rights 48–57
    see also maternity leave; preg-
        nancy
ME syndrome 74
medical reports 127–8
medical testing 9, 24–5
    and negligence 24–5
mental illness 74
minimum wage 98–105
    calculation of 99–100
    and hours worked 100–4
    making a claim 105
    obtaining information 104–5
    and sick leave 102
    and victimisation 105

minimum wage *continued*
    see also equal pay; wages
multiple sclerosis 73

negligence 137, 159
night workers 149–51
    calculating hours 151–2
    and compensatory rest 151
    definition of 150–1
    and health assessments 152–3
    and pregnancy 153
    and records of hours 152
    restrictions on 149–50
Notice of Appearance (ET3) 203,
    205
    asking for further particulars
    205–6
notice period 94, 189–90
    and guaranteed minimum pay
    190
    leaving before end of 189
    pay in lieu 191, 213
    summary dismissal during 189
    working out 190

office romances *see* relationships at
    work
output work 102–4
overtime pay
    and minimum wage 99
    and sex discrimination 48

pain, abdominal 74
parental leave 89–90
    collective/workforce agreements
    90
    fallback scheme 90
part-time workers 57–61
    equal treatment of 58
    and indirect discrimination 60,
    61
    job sharing 61
    and payment for course atten-
    dance 111–12
    protection for 57–60
    and redundancy 180–1

right to work part-time 57, 60
    and sex discrimination 59–60
    time limits for claims 60
pay systems
    and discrimination 47–8
    need to review 40–1
    and performance-related pay
    48
    and service-related benefits 47
    see also equal pay; wages
performance-related pay 48
period pains 126
personal data
    access to 130, 132–3
    inaccurate 134
    processing by employers 132,
    133–4
    protection of 131–2, 133–4
    'sensitive data' 131–2
    see also references
positive discrimination 19–20
post-natal depression 188
post-traumatic stress disorder 74
pre-hearing review 208
pre-trial directions hearing 208
pregnancy
    ante-natal appointments 54
    compensation for discrimination
    214–15
    interview questions 15
    and lifting 142
    and night work 153
    suspension on full pay 55, 56
    and unfair dismissal 39, 56–7
    workplace risk assessment 54–6,
    140
pregnancy-related sickness 50, 130,
    188–9
preliminary hearing 208
privacy, right to 122, 123–4
probationary period 35–6
productivity pay *see* performance-
    related pay
promotion 85–6
protective clothing 142–3
public duties, and time-off 112–13

race
  as genuine occupational qualifi-
    cation (GOQ) 7–8
  and positive discrimination 20
racial discrimination
  and advertisements 6
  and application forms 10–11
  and appraisals 86
  direct 61–2
  and dress codes 121
  and employment agencies 8
  and employment offers 18
  and post-employment victimisa-
    tion 71–2
  and promotion 85–6
  and redundancy 187
  and selection tests 12
  and standard of English 10, 11
  and training 86–7
recruitment 8–20
  'arrangements' 8, 9
  discrimination 8–9
'red circling' 46
redundancy 177–89
  and alternative employment 184
  'bumping' 180
  and closure of business 178
  and collective consultation
    181–3
  compensation 180, 187
  contesting 186–7
  and discrimination 187
  due to pregnancy 188–9
  and fairness 177, 179, 184–5
  going part-time 180–1
  and health record 186
  and individual consultation 183
  information from employers 182
  and job mobility 115–16, 178–9
  looking for other work 184, 189,
    215
  notice period 189
  pay entitlement 180, 181
    loss of 181, 189
  pool for selection 185
  and procedural fairness 172
  and reduction of workforce 179

selection criteria 184–8
  and trade union officials 186
  and transfer of business 178
  and unfair dismissal 177–8, 183,
    184–5
  and workplace closure 178–9
  see also dismissal
references
  challenging 21–2
  and confidentiality 20, 133,
    134
  employers' obligations 20–2
  refusal to give 22
  and truth 21, 22
relationships at work 117–18
  forbidden 118
  and gross misconduct 118
requirements or conditions 65–6
  disproportionate impact on
    women 66–9
  justification by employers 69–70,
    72
  see also indirect discrimination
resignation, and constructive dis-
    missal 174–5
rest
  breaks 154
  daily/weekly 153
  holidays 154–6
risk assessment see health and safety
  at work

salaried hours work 102
salary see gross salary
searching employees
  employers' rights 121–2
  and right to privacy 122
selection tests, and racial discrimi-
    nation 12
self-employed
  and discrimination 33
  and employment status 26, 30,
    33
  and equal pay 42
  and Maternity Allowance 53
  and minimum wage 98–9
  and working time 146

sex, as genuine occupational qualification (GOQ) 7
sex discrimination
and advertisements 5–8
and appraisals 86
and aptitude tests 13
direct 61–2
and dress codes 120–1
and employment agencies 8
and employment offers 17–19
and job descriptions 9–10
and medical information 15–16
and pay systems 47–8
and post-employment victimisation 71–2
and promotion 85–6
and redundancy 187
and shift premiums 48
and training 86–7
see also equal pay
sexual harassment 168
see also harassment
sexual orientation 82–3
shift premiums 48
sick leave 125–30
and company doctor 128
contractual sick pay 129–30
and dismissal 125, 126, 127,
128–30
long-term absences 127–9
and medical evidence 126,
127–8
and minimum wage 102
and redundancy 186
short-term absences 125–6
sickness record 15
and warnings 126
sickle cell status 25
sickness, and alternative employment 128
Small Claims Court, and Breach of
Contract 24
spinal injury 74
Statutory Maternity Pay
and not returning to work 53
qualifying for 52–3
rates 53

statutory trial period, in alternative
employment 184
stress 166–8
and disability discrimination 168
employers' obligations 166–8
and sexual harassment 168
'substantial adverse effect' 74–5
summary dismissal 176–7
during notice period 189
and unfair dismissal 177
see also dismissal; unfair dismissal
surveillance, by employers 122–3

telephone calls
collective agreement 124
monitored by employers 123–4
time work 101
time-off 108–13
for public duties 112–13
reasonable amount 113
for union activities/duties
108–12
payment for 111–12
trade union activities, time-off for
109–10
trade union duties
definition of 108
time-off for 108–9, 110–12
training union officials 109,
110–11
trade union rights
right to representation 106
union recognition 105–6
and victimisation 107–8
training 85, 86–7
transfer 85, 87
transsexuals 82

unfair dismissal 169–73
automatically unfair 105, 106,
130, 157, 194
and compensation 202, 211,
212–13
for dress/appearance 119
and fixed-term contracts 33–4
and interim relief 106

and sickness 129–30
and termination of contract 93, 94
for trade union activities 106
waiving right to claim 34
for whistleblowing 194, 195
see also constructive dismissal; dismissal
uniform
and racial discrimination 121
and sex discrimination 119
unmeasured work 104

victimisation
and minimum wage 105
post-employment 71–2
protection from 70–1
and trade union membership 107–8
violence at work 157–8
risk assessment 158
voyeurism 74

wages
deductions 94–5, 96–7
definition of 95–6
errors in 97, 98
reduction in 96
see also equal pay; minimum wage; pay systems
whistleblowing 191–5
gagging clauses 194
on health and safety issues 194–5
for infringement of rights 195
procedure 193
protected disclosures 192–4
and unfair dismissal 194, 195
and victimisation 194, 195
workers not protected 192
witnesses 206–7
statements from 207

women
and child-care responsibilities 65, 66, 69
complying with requirements 66–9
from overseas 36–8
and health and safety at work 136
and lifting 141, 142
and part-time work 57
training 19–20
and violence at work 157
work place risk assessment 54–6, 140
'work of equal value' 45
'work rated as equivalent' 43, 45
working time
calculating hours 100–4, 149, 151–2
definition of 146–7
enforcing rights 156–7
exclusions from regulation 146, 150
maximum 147–8, 149–50
and night work 149–51
records of 148, 152
and travelling time 103, 104
and workforce agreements 147, 150
see also annual leave; night workers; part-time workers; rest
wrongful dismissal 175–6
see also dismissal; unfair dismissal

Zero Hours Contracts, and employment rights 35

Compiled by Sue Carlton